GRAPPLE

jr. high

12 LESSONS

TACKLING TOUGH QUESTIONS ABOUT GOD, OTHERS, AND ME

HOPE IN A HOPELESS WORLD

CD & DVD INCLUDED

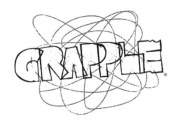

Grapple® Jr. High: Hope in a Hopeless World
Copyright © 2011 Group Publishing, Inc.

group.com
simplyyouthministry.com

ISBN 978-0-7644-7547-4

10 9 8 7 6 5 4 3 2 1   20 19 18 17 16 15 14 13 12 11

Printed in the United States of America.

TABLE OF CONTENTS

INTRODUCTION

GRAPPLE® JR. HIGH

Some of your students may already seem jaded about the Bible, and some of them have never cracked one open. Wherever your teenagers are in their spiritual journey, two things they all have in common are an inquisitive mind and a need for Christ-centered biblical depth. Grapple Jr. High is specifically designed to get junior highers grappling with tough topics in meaningful ways so they understand and own their faith. Each week, students engage with memorable Bible passages and characters, grapple with the issues that come to the surface, and discover a path that leads them straight to Jesus Christ.

During class, students follow the same schedule each week.

GRAPPLE SCHEDULE

5 MINUTES	HANG TIME
10 MINUTES	GRAPPLE CHAT
10-15 MINUTES	GRAPPLE TIME
20-25 MINUTES	TEAM TIME
10 MINUTES	TEAM REPORTS
5 MINUTES	PRAYER & CHALLENGE

Please note that times are approximate and should be flexible to fit your classroom needs.

WHAT HAPPENS?
GRAPPLE HANG TIME:

Kids enjoy snacks and friendship as they spend time getting to know each other as music plays in the background. Then play a three-minute countdown, included on your Grapple DVD, to let students know how much time they have until Grapple Hang Time is over. You can also use the countdowns to wrap up an activity in the lesson.

GRAPPLE CHAT:

Chat topics connect students to one another and to the Word of God. Two topics in each lesson are built on passages or characters from the Bible, and two topics challenge students to discuss their lives. Encourage students to choose one question from each of these categories. In each lesson, Questions 1 and 3 are the biblically based questions, and Questions 2 and 4 are the ones that tap into their personal experiences.

GRAPPLE TIME:

Grapple Time is the leader-led experience for your entire class. Grapple Time involves everyone in making discoveries; the experience helps students cultivate the desire to dig into the Bible for answers.

GRAPPLE TEAM TIME:

Students get into their Grapple Teams of six or fewer to dig into the Bible with the reproducible Grapple Team Guide.

Who leads a Grapple Team? If you have six or fewer students, have them stay together with you as the leader. If you have several Grapple Teams, try these ideas: Facilitate all the teams by moving from team to team, assign a student to be the team leader, or recruit adults or high school students to be team leaders.

GRAPPLE TEAM REPORTS:

Teams vote on how they want to report what they discovered during Grapple Team Time. Once teams are ready to report, they get with other teams that chose the other style of reporting. They then take turns reporting what they learned. If you have just one Grapple Team, consider dividing your team into two smaller groups to create and present reports.

GRAPPLE PRAYER AND CHALLENGE:

Kids choose, as a class, which prayer option they would like to do. After the class closes in prayer, give kids the weekly Grapple Challenge to live out their faith during the coming week.

ALLERGY ALERT

This guide may contain activities that include food. Be aware that some kids have food allergies that can be dangerous. Know the students in your class, and consult with parents about allergies their kids may have. Also be sure to carefully read food labels, as hidden ingredients can cause allergy-related problems.

HEAVEN AND HELL

IS HEAVEN GOING TO BE BORING?

HEAVEN AND HELL

Is Heaven Going to Be Boring?
The Point: Heaven Will Be a Grand Adventure
The Passages: Isaiah 65:17-19; 1 Peter 1:3-4; Revelation 4:1-11

GET STARTED
Lesson 1. Is Heaven Going to Be Boring?

GRAPPLE SCHEDULE

5 MINUTES	HANG TIME
10 MINUTES	GRAPPLE CHAT
10-15 MINUTES	GRAPPLE TIME
20-25 MINUTES	TEAM TIME
10 MINUTES	TEAM REPORTS
5 MINUTES	PRAYER & CHALLENGE

SUPPLIES
Bibles, Grapple DVD, DVD player, music CD, CD player, copy of the Grapple Team Guide for each person, paper, pens or pencils, chenille wires (also referred to as craft pipe cleaners), modeling dough or clay

BIBLE BASIS FOR TEACHERS
The Passage: Revelation 4:1-11

John's vision of God on the throne is simple and similar to visions from the Old Testament (see Isaiah 6 and Ezekiel 1). The vision, however, does convey the majesty and supremacy of God Almighty. In addition to describing God's majesty, John describes how people and other living beings respond to that majestic presence. Day after day and night after night they keep on saying, "Holy, holy, holy is the Lord God, the Almighty—the one who always was, who is, and who is to come" (Revelation 4:8). John's vision reveals that in heaven God will be forever present and that the natural impulse of anyone in the presence of God will be to worship God.

When Isaiah experienced a similar vision (see Isaiah 6:1-4), he responded by saying, "It's all over! I am doomed, for I am a sinful man. I have filthy lips, and I live among a people with filthy lips. Yet I have seen the King, the Lord of Heaven's Armies" (Isaiah 6:5). For Isaiah, being in God's presence as a sinner was frightening. John, however, is not afraid the way Isaiah was.

How does this relate to the Grapple Question? The illustrations that Scripture provides present heaven as a place where we will gather with the multitudes and worship God forever—in other words, an eternal church service. Some kids don't mind going to church once or twice a week, while others count the seconds

until church is over, but few people want to sit in church 24/7. This idea may seem more like hell than heaven to some. This week's Grapple Question will help students envision the glory of God and his dwelling place.

John provides a colorful and poetic revelation of the glory he experienced. But while John's vision is exciting and may make for a cool scene in a movie, it doesn't capture the ultimate greatness that heaven promises us. The Bible is written in human language, which is incapable of fully describing the adventure that waits in heaven. If Steven Spielberg had received the same vision, he likely would have portrayed heaven differently. The truth is that in heaven we will be in the immediate presence of God, and unlike Isaiah, we won't have to be afraid. And that will be indescribably majestic, brilliant, and adventuresome.

How does this connect to Jesus? It is through Jesus that this connection to God is even possible. Immediately after describing God's heavenly throne in Revelation 4, John tells of his vision of a lamb opening a scroll in the right hand of God. The Lamb is the only one worthy to open the scroll because he "has won the victory" (Revelation 5:5). Because of Jesus—the lamb—we can all approach the one who sits on the throne. By believing in Jesus, we can experience the ultimate adventure of heaven and God's glory.

GRAPPLE HANG TIME: 5 MINUTES
Play music as kids enjoy snacks and friendship; then play an opening countdown from the Grapple DVD to wrap up Grapple Hang Time.

GRAPPLE CHAT: 10 MINUTES
Have students form pairs; if you have an uneven number of kids, it's OK to have one trio in the mix. Ask each group to chat about two of the four topics below that relate to today's grapple topic. (Answers in parentheses are samples.)

IN PAIRS
Chat 1: According to the book of Genesis, what was the maximum number of years that God gave man to live? (120 years, Genesis 6:3)

Chat 2: What's the most number of people you've ever had over for a party?

Chat 3: Find a person in the Bible who was extremely happy about something. (Jacob and Esau reconciled, Genesis 33:4; the people when the new Temple was built, Ezra 3:12)

Chat 4: People talk about the "seven wonders of the world." From your perspective, what's the "eighth wonder of the world"?

GRAPPLE TIME: 10-15 MINUTES
Get Ready: Cue the Grapple DVD to the "Heavenly Tours" clip.

Lead the entire class in the following:

Form teams of three, and give each team a handful of chenille wires (also sometime referred to as craft pipe cleaners).

The word paradise comes from a Greek word meaning "fun park." Today we're going to turn the classroom into a theme park called "Paradise." Your job is to design a fun-filled ride for our park and sculpt it with your chenille wires. Be creative! And don't forget to give your thrill ride a catchy name.

Have teams work for a few minutes; then get their attention.

I'm sure you've designed an action-packed fun park together. Now let's take a tour of "Paradise." Take turns showing us your ride, telling us what it's called and how it works.

TELL ALL
How does your ride fit into the theme of paradise? What do all of the rides have in common? What does this activity suggest about the way we define "fun"? Where do you think people get their thirst for joy and excitement?

IN PAIRS
King David was a guy who knew how to have a good time. Read Psalm 43:3-4 with your partner. What is David's idea of paradise? What is your greatest joy and delight in life? Which is more important to you: enjoying pleasure or avoiding pain? Why?

Let's watch a video to explore this more deeply.

Show the "Heavenly Tours" clip on the Grapple DVD.

There are some really exciting things for us to enjoy about our world. In fact, some people see the descriptions of heaven in some parts of the Bible as less interesting than a good day at a local theme park. Will heaven be a letdown? Sure, it might be nice to live in a city with jasper walls and golden streets, but what kind of reward is that anyway? Let's grapple with that!

GRAPPLE TEAM TIME: 20-25 MINUTES
Break into Grapple Teams. Encourage Grapple Team leaders to check in with kids about their week. Grapple Team leaders will facilitate discussion, using the Grapple Team Guide on pages 7-8. Afterward, students will report what they learned.

GRAPPLE TEAM REPORTS: 10 MINUTES
At the end of Grapple Team Time, match Grapple Teams that chose Option 1 with Grapple Teams that chose Option 2 from page 8. Have teams present their reports.

(If you have an uneven number of teams, simply form one group of three teams for the presentations. If you have only two Grapple Teams, simply do the presentations one team at a time.)

GRAPPLE PRAYER AND CHALLENGE: 5 MINUTES

Read the Grapple Prayer options. Have the class choose one prayer option that everyone will do. Allow students time to pray about what they discovered. Then close in prayer.

Option 1: Word Prayers

Take a quiet moment to consider what you know about God. Then prayerfully call out one or two words that describe who God is, such as Comforter, Protector, Provider, or Shepherd.

Option 2: Lectio Divina

Get comfortable, preferably sitting apart from each other. Read a Bible passage aloud, and then remain in silence for a few minutes and think about the verses. Close your eyes and breathe deeply. Then read aloud Romans 8:35-39, slowly and with feeling. Then read it two more times the same way. Finally, allow a few minutes to silently bask in God's love.

GRAPPLE CHALLENGE

All the fun things we do in life come from a deeper hunger inside of us. When we get together with friends to play games, eat at a restaurant, or watch a movie, we are searching to fulfill deeper needs such as joy and peace. The same loving God who gave us those desires also has given us the present hope of being full of joy forever through Jesus. Getting closer to God is getting closer to true joy. That's what heaven is all about! You'll face challenges and persecutions that will make you doubt whether heaven is worth it. But I challenge you to drop the shallow definitions of heaven and replace them with something true—a place where the greatest adventures of all time happen.

WEEKLY GRAPPLE CONNECTION
Grapple Question: Is Heaven Going to Be Boring?
Kids Learn: Heaven Will Be a Grand Adventure
Dig Into the Bible: Revelation 4:1-11

What do you imagine heaven will be like? Do you think of a constant party atmosphere, a quiet peaceful waterfall, or a never-ending worship service? In Isaiah 65:19, God gives us a little glimpse of what it will be like: "I will rejoice over Jerusalem and delight in my people. And the sound of weeping and crying will be heard in it no more."

During tough times when our faith is being tested, we might sometimes wonder if heaven will be worth it. Keep focused by talking as a family about what heaven will be like. Does your idea of paradise include unlimited ice cream, lots of space for running around and playing together, and constant laughter? (And don't forget to talk about what won't be there: grief, loneliness, your job, and whiney pets!) The one thing we know for sure is that we will be praising God a lot. Tonight practice that as a family by singing a favorite worship song together or talking about your individual visions of heaven.

- -

GRAPPLE TEAM GUIDE LESSON 1

In your Grapple Team, use this guide to grapple with today's question.

Often, when people try to explain something really awesome, they use creatively descriptive language. For instance, a person might describe a great fireworks show as "eye-popping" or a tasty piece of cake as "something to die for." The same thing happens in the passage we're about to read. But before we read it, let's look at some good examples from the Bible. See if you can spot the colorful expressions in each of these passages.

Matthew 5:29 _____.

Psalm 61:3 _____.

Deuteronomy 4:24 _____.

Read Revelation 4:1-11

IN PAIRS

Obviously the writer of this passage is trying to describe what is, for him, the fulfillment of joy, worship, and eternal rest with God. With a partner, do your best to describe the following situations in fewer than 20 words.

Describe the view of earth from space:

_____

_____

Describe what it's like to ride an angry rhinoceros:

_____

_____

Describe your idea of heaven:

_____

_____

IN PAIRS

What was the toughest part about putting these situations into words? How is your idea of heaven different from the one in the passage? You may not see yourself placing crowns at the feet of God, but how do you imagine yourself worshipping God in heaven?

Read Isaiah 65:17-19

In many ways, heaven is like an eternal trip to God's theme park. Based on this passage, come up with a sentence that illustrates what you'd expect to find in this "place of happiness."

_____

_____

Take turns sharing your sentences with your Grapple Team. The passage from Isaiah promises eternal happiness, but as you listen to what others imagine about heaven, close your eyes and try to visualize what they're describing.

IN PAIRS

What kinds of things did others consider that you did not? How do these sentences change the way you visualize heaven?

Read aloud 1 Peter 1:3-4

According to this passage, the reason for our "great expectation" is our inheritance that can never decay. List a few items that have been handed down in your family (jewelry, pictures, or furniture, for example).

_____

_____

In what way do the words and actions of Jesus on earth give us a preview of what heaven looks like? Why is it so difficult to find things in life that are "beyond the reach of change and decay"?

GRAPPLE TEAM REPORTS

With your team, choose one of the options below to report what you discovered.

Get Ready: For Option 2, distribute modeling dough or clay.

Option 1: Condense It
If you had to summarize today's lesson in only five words, what would they be? As a team, choose the words carefully, and be prepared to explain why you chose them.

Option 2: Sculpt It
Take some modeling dough or clay, and sculpt objects that explain or reveal what you discovered today. Be prepared to interpret your artwork in case you tend to create abstract art!

IS HEAVEN GOING TO BE BORING?
(STUDENT)

Revelation 4:8b
"Holy, holy, holy is the Lord God, the Almighty—the one who always was, who is, and who is still to come."

GRAPPLE CHAT
Chat 1: According to the book of Genesis, what was the maximum number of years that God gave man to live?

Chat 2: What's the most number of people you've ever had over for a party?

Chat 3: Find a person in the Bible who was extremely happy about something.

Chat 4: People talk about the "seven wonders of the world." From your perspective, what's the "eighth wonder of the world"?

GRAPPLE CHALLENGE
Whenever you're having fun this week, consider the fact that heaven will be better than anything you can experience here on earth.

NOTES:

_____

_____

_____

_____

_____

_____

_____

_____

HEAVEN AND HELL

ISN'T ANY GOD ENOUGH?

HEAVEN AND HELL

Isn't Any God Enough?
The Point: Jesus Is the Only Way
The Passages: Psalm 18:16-19; John 14:1-14; Romans 1:18-23; 2:12-16

GET STARTED
Lesson 2. Isn't Any God Enough?

GRAPPLE SCHEDULE

5 MINUTES	HANG TIME
10 MINUTES	GRAPPLE CHAT
10-15 MINUTES	GRAPPLE TIME
20-25 MINUTES	TEAM TIME
10 MINUTES	TEAM REPORTS
5 MINUTES	PRAYER & CHALLENGE

SUPPLIES
Bibles, Grapple DVD, DVD player, music CD, CD player, copy of the Grapple Team Guide for each person, paper, pens or pencils, whiteboard and dry-erase markers (or newsprint/butcher paper and permanent markers), several dictionaries or printed definitions of *truth* from an online dictionary, small pieces of masking tape, markers

BIBLE BASIS FOR TEACHERS
The Passage: John 14:1-14
Prior to this passage, Jesus prepared himself and his disciples for the most painful and trying point of his ministry. Jesus modeled true servanthood when he washed his disciples' feet. He predicted his betrayal by Judas, he predicted Peter's denial, and he told his disciples that he would be leaving them. He did encourage them, however, to trust in God and to not be troubled.

Jesus told his disciples that they should know the way to where he was going. But time and time again, Jesus' disciples had a difficult time understanding who Jesus really was, and Jesus sometimes expressed frustration because they didn't really know him. On this occasion, Thomas came right out and said, "We have no idea where you are going, so how can we know the way?" Jesus answered Thomas with one of his most famous "I am" statements: "I am the way, the truth, and the life. No one can come to the Father except through me."

How does this relate to the Grapple Question? In this passage, Jesus made a bold statement that would forever impact the fabric of Christianity. Jesus didn't just claim to be one of many ways to experience God or to have full access to

enlightenment. Nor did he claim to offer one of many ways to attain everlasting life. In fact, Jesus made an exclusive statement; it's either his way or the highway. The only way you can have access to God is by believing in Jesus Christ. In this passage Jesus also said, "If you had really known me, you would know who my Father is." True access to God comes through believing in Jesus and really knowing who he is.

How does this connect to Jesus? What does Jesus mean when he claims to be the way? Some of the disciples were confused because, as Jesus put it, they didn't really know him. Jesus isn't a cosmic tour guide who directs people into the presence of God. Knowing Jesus is the way to God because Jesus is God. Jesus states in this passage that he is in the Father and the Father is in him. There is no way to know God other than through Jesus because Jesus is God. For thousands of years before the coming of Jesus, people tried to get close to God. But no matter how hard they tried, they could never get close enough to God because a holy God could not be in the presence of sinful people. However, by coming to people in the person of Jesus, God provides all sinful people with a "way" to dwell in his presence. Therefore, the only way to really get to know God is to get to know Jesus.

GRAPPLE HANG TIME: 5 MINUTES
Play music as kids enjoy snacks and friendship; then play an opening countdown from the Grapple DVD to wrap up Grapple Hang Time.

GRAPPLE CHAT
Have students form pairs; if you have an uneven number of kids, it's OK to have one trio in the mix. Ask each group to chat about two of the four topics below that relate to today's grapple topic. (Answers in parentheses are samples.)

IN PAIRS
Chat 1: Find a Bible verse that shows someone changing travel plans suddenly. (Paul on his way to Damascus, Acts 9:1-12; Jonah and Nineveh, Jonah 3:1-3)

Chat 2: How far do you travel to get to church? Do you always travel the same route, or does your family take a variety of different routes?

Chat 3: According to the Bible, what group of people holds the record for being "lost" for the longest amount of time? (The Israelites, Numbers 32:13)

Chat 4: How many states have you visited? Which one was your favorite, and why?

GRAPPLE TIME: 10-15 MINUTES
Get Ready: Cue the Grapple DVD to the "All Roads" clip.

Write the phrase "gzikdn ebuhncenzar fablo anoyb" in large letters on a whiteboard or large piece of butcher paper where everyone can see it—or be prepared to read the letters aloud to students and have them write the jumbled words on their handouts. Then write, "Ezra 5:12" on four small strips of paper and fold them up.

Form four groups and hand a Bible, pencils, and some paper to each group. Then lead the entire class in the following:

I want you all to work together to figure out the four words in this scrambled phrase. It shouldn't take too long if you try really hard.

It's likely your students won't unscramble the phrase quickly. After just a couple of minutes, call someone from one of the groups to go outside the room (so others won't overhear). Hand him or her one of the strips of paper, saying, "This is the way." Send the person back inside, and repeat the process with a member of another group, until all four groups have solved the anagram (King Nebuchadnezzar of Babylon).

IN PAIRS

How did it feel to try solving the puzzle without any clues? What were you thinking when someone from your group went out of the room? What would have been different if that person had never come back?

In life, there are often several ways to do things—and most of the time, people choose the easiest way. Now, on a blank sheet of paper, write out two different sets of directions from here to your favorite restaurant in town. Then team up with a partner and swap your papers. Determine which of your sets of directions is easier.

TELL ALL

How did you decide which way was easier? When have you recently had to choose between different ways of doing things in your life? How did your choices turn out?

Let's watch a video to see more about this.

Show the "All Roads" clip on the Grapple DVD.

With so many nations and cultures all over the world, is it just our arrogance that makes us think Jesus is the only way to God? Are there "good people" who aren't Christians? As long as you believe in a god, any god, isn't that enough? Get your gloves on because we just may have to dig really deep to grapple with this question!

GRAPPLE TEAM TIME: 20-25 MINUTES

Break into Grapple Teams. Encourage Grapple Team leaders to check in with kids about their week. Grapple Team leaders will facilitate discussion, using the Grapple Team Guide on pages 17-19. Afterward, students will report what they learned.

GRAPPLE TEAM REPORTS: 10 MINUTES

At the end of Grapple Team Time, match Grapple Teams that chose Option 1 with Grapple Teams that chose Option 2 from page 19. Have teams present their reports.

(If you have an uneven number of teams, simply form one group of three teams for the presentations. If you have only two Grapple Teams, simply do the presentations one team at a time.)

GRAPPLE PRAYER AND CHALLENGE: 5 MINUTES

Read the Grapple Prayer options. Have the class choose one prayer option that everyone will do. Allow students time to pray about what they discovered. Then close in prayer.

Get Ready: For Option 2, distribute markers and small pieces of masking tape.

Option 1: Quiet Prayers

Spread out around the room, and get comfortable so you won't be distracted by others. Psalm 143:10 begins with, "Teach me to do your will." Pray that simple phrase over and over, slowly and quietly, and listen for what the Holy Spirit wants to teach you today. Write down any thoughts or ideas that come to mind as you listen.

Option 2: Sticky Situations

Write one of your weaknesses on a small piece of masking tape. Put the tape on your arm, leg, or face. Then pray, asking God to be strong in your weakness. Ask God to speak up for you as your enemy tries to hurt you.

GRAPPLE CHALLENGE

In a society where we are loaded down with choices and encouraged to find our own path, it's tempting to think you can replace God with other things. But remember that there is one God, one truth, and one perfect example of total fulfillment in life: Jesus. So this week, I challenge you to walk away from second-rate pleasures when they lead you away from doing the right things. The world can be a scary place, but when Jesus is with us, we always have the strength to face our fears and temptations.

WEEKLY GRAPPLE CONNECTION
Grapple Question: Isn't Any God Enough?
Kids Learn: Jesus Is the Only Way
Dig Into the Bible: John 14:1-14

When was the last time you were lost? Or worse, accidentally separated from your kids (maybe in a store or other public place)? Being lost can be terrifying.

People who are spiritually lost may experience the same panic or feeling of emptiness. And the need to quiet the panic or fill the emptiness can cause them to look in the wrong places: Drugs, alcohol, work, and even TV can drown out feelings of fear and loneliness for a while. But looking in those places won't bring true contentment because Jesus is the only way to true peace in life.

Who in your life is spiritually lost? Send an email or make a quick phone call to reach out to that person with compassion and empathy. Encourage your son or daughter to do the same with a friend. Pray with your child each morning that all your friends will find true peace through a relationship with Jesus.

- -

GRAPPLE TEAM GUIDE LESSON 2
In your Grapple Team, use this guide to grapple with today's question.

Imagine you're lost in a forest and traveling on a well-worn trail. Suddenly you discover a less-traveled path marked with a sign indicating that the path leads to a town. Would you continue plodding through the woods, or would you choose the less-traveled path? Why? Describe a time in your life when you felt lost— misunderstanding your parents or being confused in math class, for example. Then describe what happened to make you feel better.

_____

_____

Read Psalm 18:16-19

IN PAIRS
According to David, God rescued him from deep waters and powerful enemies. When have you experienced this type of help from God in your own life? How has God helped you deal with your fears?

_____

_____

What kinds of "rescue" can only God provide? What evidence do you have from the Bible that God is concerned about rescuing us from trouble?

_____

_____

Get Ready

Distribute dictionaries or printed definitions of truth from an online dictionary; if you choose the printed definitions, do not distribute until after students have created their own person definitions of truth.

We often use the word _truth_ without knowing what we mean. Write out a definition for _truth_. Then, when everyone on your team has done that, have someone read the definition of _truth_ from a dictionary.

_____

_____

IN PAIRS

Whose definition was closest—yours or your partner's? Is the dictionary definition of _truth_ different from how the Bible would define it? Explain. If it's true that there is only one God, do you think there is more than one "truth" or more than one "way"? Why or why not?

_____

_____

Read John 14:1-14

In this passage, Thomas and Philip had some questions for Jesus about what was going to happen next in their lives. Write down a few "burning questions" that you'd ask Jesus if he were literally sitting beside you right now.

_____

_____

Based on Jesus' words in this passage, can a person find truth through other gods? Why or why not? What's one way your questions to Jesus would be different from those of a person who had never heard of Christianity?

_____

_____

Read Romans 1:18-23; 2:12-16

In the space below, respond to the following statement: "Christians are arrogant to think that their way is the only way." When finished, discuss your response with your Grapple Team.

_____

_____

GRAPPLE TEAM REPORTS

With your team, choose one of the options below to report what you discovered.

Option 1: Project Youth!

With your team, choose your three best ideas about how you could help the youth group learn about today's lesson and put its truths into practice. Be prepared to explain why these truths are important for teenagers to believe and follow.

Option 2: ABCs

Write the ABCs of what you learned today: a statement that starts with an A, a statement that starts with a B, and so on. Try to go as far into the alphabet as you can—even all the way to Z.

ISN'T ANY GOD ENOUGH?

Revelation 4:8b
"Holy, holy, holy is the Lord God, the Almighty—the one who always was, who is, and who is still to come."

GRAPPLE CHAT

Chat 1: Find a Bible verse that shows someone changing travel plans suddenly.

Chat 2: How far do you travel to get to church? Do you always travel the same route, or does your family take a variety of different routes?

Chat 3: According to the Bible, what group of people holds the record for being "lost" for the longest amount of time?

Chat 4: How many states have you visited? Which one was your favorite, and why?

GRAPPLE CHALLENGE

Sometime this week, when you're faced with a decision, choose the toughest option and then ask God to help you with this difficult decision—especially when that means walking away from second-rate pleasures because they lead you away from doing the right things.

NOTES:

_____

_____

_____

_____

_____

_____

_____

HEAVEN AND HELL

DOES GOD SEND PEOPLE TO HELL?

HEAVEN AND HELL

Does God Send People to Hell?
The Point: God Honors Our Freedom to Choose
The Passages: Matthew 12:40; 1 Timothy 2:6; 2 Peter 3:3-16

GET STARTED
Lesson 3. Does God Send People to Hell?

GRAPPLE SCHEDULE

5 MINUTES	HANG TIME
10 MINUTES	GRAPPLE CHAT
10-15 MINUTES	GRAPPLE TIME
20-25 MINUTES	TEAM TIME
10 MINUTES	TEAM REPORTS
5 MINUTES	PRAYER & CHALLENGE

SUPPLIES
Bibles, Grapple DVD, DVD player, music CD, CD player, copy of the Grapple Team Guide for each person, paper, pens or pencils, several obituaries cut from newspapers, bull's-eye

BIBLE BASIS FOR TEACHERS
The Passage: 2 Peter 3:3-16

In this passage, Peter reaffirms God's promises to his people. Apparently, false teachers were already rising up to deny the promises of Jesus' return as well as the concept of judgment. Many false prophets and teachers were telling the people of the church that, since a significant amount of time had already passed and Jesus had not returned, he would never return. Peter assures the church that God does keep his promises, he will judge the world, and Jesus will return. Peter writes that God isn't being slow to keep his promises; he's just being merciful and patient with those who have not yet repented.

Peter reminded the people of his day that God does not work within the time frame we have on earth and that God is waiting for all people to turn toward him because God truly wants everyone to be saved. Peter knew, and reminded the church, that Jesus would return unexpectedly. With that in mind, Peter encouraged people to continue to choose God over unrighteousness. God may be waiting for all people to repent, but eventually the end will come. At this end, those who are righteous will be judged alongside those who are unrighteous.

How does this relate to the Grapple Question? Teenagers (and adults) frequently grapple with this question: How can a loving God send people to hell?

This passage assures us that God is a loving God and doesn't send anyone to hell. However, God gave humans the freedom to choose whether or not to pursue him. Second Peter 3:9 assures us that God, out of love and mercy, is patiently waiting for people to seek him. God doesn't want anyone to go to hell. However, if people choose to ignore God's invitation, God will honor that decision. Heaven is spending eternity with God, and hell is the exact opposite of that. If someone chooses to be in a place devoid of God, God honors that person's freedom to choose.

How does this connect to Jesus? Jesus is the open invitation. To pursue Jesus is to pursue God. Anyone who makes a decision to follow Christ has accepted God's invitation into heaven. God is waiting patiently for all people to choose to follow Jesus because God wants all people to experience forgiveness and salvation. The coming of Jesus is ultimately the sign and seal of God's love for humanity. God sent Jesus to die to save humanity, and God desires all human beings to choose to love him in return (see John 3:16-17).

GRAPPLE HANG TIME: 5 MINUTES
Play music as kids enjoy snacks and friendship; then play an opening countdown from the Grapple DVD to wrap up Grapple Hang Time.

GRAPPLE CHAT
Have students form pairs; if you have an uneven number of kids, it's OK to have one trio in the mix. Ask each group to chat about two of the four topics below that relate to today's grapple topic. (Answers in parentheses are samples.)

IN PAIRS
Chat 1: Find at least two verses that mention hell. (Matthew 7:13; Romans 8:38)

Chat 2: What was the most significant decision you've made recently, and why was it such an important decision?

Chat 3: Name a Bible story that tells about two brothers making very different choices. (Jacob and Esau, Genesis 28:1-9; Cain and Abel, Genesis 4:3-5)

Chat 4: When was the last time you built or helped build a fire? Was it an enjoyable or frustrating experience?

GRAPPLE TIME: 10-15 MINUTES

Get Ready: Cue the Grapple DVD to the "Choices" clip.

Clear some floor space for kids to lie down, and lead the entire class in the following:

Today we're going to be storytellers. Get into your Grapple Teams, and take a minute to choose a popular fairy tale or book or TV show or movie that portrays a character making a bad choice. You will illustrate this story by having each member of your team play a character or role.

Observe as teams choose their stories; if some are struggling, help them to decide quickly, in the interest of time. (Some suggestions of fairy tales include Little Red Riding Hood, The Gingerbread Man, or The Three Little Pigs.) Once the scenes are ready, choose a team to go first, while the "readers" (audience) sit on the floor to watch. Roughly midway through each presentation, stop the group and re-assign roles at random so that, without their choosing to do so, team members are all playing new roles.

IN PAIRS
How did it feel to suddenly have no choice in what role you were playing? What would life be like if someone were always forcing you to do things you didn't want to do? Would it bother you for the group to illustrate one of the most regrettable choices you've made in your life? Why or why not?

TELL ALL
What were some consequences of the choices these characters made? What are some consequences of choices you make every day?

Let's watch a video to see more about this.

Show the "Choices" clip on the Grapple DVD.

I know it seems like a contradiction, but being free is actually a responsibility. We're free to choose things in our lives, but such freedom demands that we try to make good choices. When "forever" is on the line, we can feel a lot of pressure to get things right—or else! But what kinds of people really go to hell? Could we be heading there—and not know it? Let's grapple with that!

GRAPPLE TEAM TIME: 20-25 MINUTES
Break into Grapple Teams. Encourage Grapple Team leaders to check in with kids about their week. Grapple Team leaders will facilitate discussion, using the Grapple Team Guide on pages 29-30. Afterward, students will report what they learned.

GRAPPLE TEAM REPORTS: 10 MINUTES
At the end of Grapple Team Time, match Grapple Teams that chose Option 1 with Grapple Teams that chose Option 2 from page 31. Have teams present their reports.

(If you have an uneven number of teams, simply form one group of three teams for the presentations. If you have only two Grapple Teams, simply do the presentations one team at a time.)

GRAPPLE PRAYER AND CHALLENGE: 5 MINUTES

Read the Grapple Prayer options. Have the class choose one prayer option that everyone will do. Allow students time to pray about what they discovered. Then close in prayer.

Get Ready

For Option 2, affix the bull's-eye to the far wall, and distribute paper to students.

Option 1: Still Small Voice

Close your eyes and think about one difficult thing you're currently going through. Ask God to show you where he is in this situation. After a period of reflective silence, ask God what he is trying to say to you through this circumstance. Write down any thoughts or ideas that come to mind.

Option 2: Marksman, Markswoman

Make paper airplanes, and take turns throwing the airplanes at the bull's-eye. Walk to wherever your airplane lands and pray to God about one way you miss the mark in your life. Relate what you say to what you learned today.

GRAPPLE CHALLENGE

From the beginning, humans have tried to blame others for their own bad choices. Adam blamed Eve, and Eve blamed the serpent. Now, because of the death and resurrection of Jesus, your destination is up to you. You can decide if you will accept that heaven and hell are real places meant for people who have made very different choices. God loves you and wants you to be with him forever, but God will not interfere with the choices you make. And although the choices are yours, God is always near you, willing to help you, forgive you, and challenge your faith. That is the good news; that is the gospel!

WEEKLY GRAPPLE CONNECTION

Grapple Question: Does God Send People to Hell?
Kids Learn: God Honors Our Freedom to Choose
Dig Into the Bible: 2 Peter 3:3-16

Life is really all about choices, isn't it? You've been giving your child the opportunity to make choices since you let her choose her own outfit at age 2 or since you gave him breakfast-cereal options when he was a toddler. And now that you're raising a young teenager, you're providing more and more opportunities for your child to make decisions.

Teaching teenagers to make wise decisions isn't just preparation for adulthood. It's also preparation for eternity. Because God gives us the freedom to choose to follow him, your child will have the responsibility of making the one choice that matters most.

Praise your child for making a wise decision this week. Spend a few moments praying for your teenager. Ask God to help your child make wise decisions, and ask God to give you the strength to be a good example as a parent. God honors your requests and faithfulness.

- -

GRAPPLE TEAM GUIDE LESSON 3
In your Grapple Team, use this guide to grapple with today's question.

We all have a lot of freedom in our lives to choose things for ourselves. Consider the freedoms listed below and rank them from 1 to 9, assigning "1" to the freedom you value the most, and so on.

The freedom to choose my:

___ Name	___ Food	___ Clothes
___ Career	___ Place to Live	___ Friends
___ Height	___ Hair Color	___ I.Q.

IN PAIRS
Compare your lists, and circle any freedoms that you both ranked high or both ranked low. In what ways do the freedoms you value in common tell something about your personalities? Are there any other freedoms that you would have ranked high that aren't on the list? If so, what are they? How would your parents have rearranged your list?

Many people use the terms *heaven* and *hell*, but it's difficult to describe where these places actually are. Take a moment to draw a picture of the earth, including heaven and hell. Label all three clearly, and then, just for kicks, draw a tiny picture of yourself on the earth!

Read Matthew 12:40 and 1 Timothy 2:6

IN PAIRS

According to 1 Timothy, we are responsible for choosing our path. Jesus purchased freedom for everyone by giving his life on the cross. What kinds of things would you be willing to give your life for? What do you think it means that this good news was given at "just the right time"?

How does your drawing of hell match up with Matthew 12:40? Where would you put the "Son of Man" in your drawing of the earth? What does it mean to you that he was there so you don't have to be?

Get Ready

Distribute the obituaries cut from newspapers.

Read 2 Peter 3:3-16

Using this passage and an example obituary, write out an obituary for the world. Include some of the significant good and bad things that have happened here on the earth, and say something about what will happen next.

_____

_____

_____

_____

_____

_____

Based on 2 Peter 3:9, God is not slow—but patient. What does that patience say about the character of God and God's love for everyone? Do people's choices increase or decrease God's love for them? If your own obituary was written tomorrow, what are the things you would be most proud of? disappointed about?

GRAPPLE TEAM REPORTS

With your team, choose one of the options below to report what you discovered.

Option 1: New Perspective

Talk about how today's lesson has changed your perspective on heaven and hell. And then get a new physical perspective: Stand on a table, stand on your head, stretch out on the floor—whatever you want! Hold that position as one member of your team explains how today's lesson has provided a new perspective. Do a "test run" as a team before making your presentation to the other team.

Option 2: Knowit Poets!

Write a poem or a rap about what you learned today, making every sentence contain the word *heaven*—or a word that rhymes with it.

DOES GOD SEND PEOPLE TO HELL?

Revelation 4:8b
"Holy, holy, holy is the Lord God, the Almighty—the one who always was, who is, and who is still to come."

GRAPPLE CHAT
Chat 1: Find at least two verses that mention hell.

Chat 2: What was the most significant decision you've made recently, and why was it such an important decision?

Chat 3: Name a Bible story that tells about two brothers making very different choices.

Chat 4: When was the last time you built or helped build a fire? Was it an enjoyable or frustrating experience?

GRAPPLE CHALLENGE
Every night this week, before you go to bed, spend five minutes thanking Jesus for experiencing hell so that you don't have to.

NOTES:

_____

_____

_____

_____

_____

_____

_____

HEAVEN
AND HELL

IS HELL REALLY
THAT BAD?

HEAVEN AND HELL

Is Hell Really That Bad?
The Point: Hell Is Separation From God
The Passages: Exodus 34:6; Psalm 22:1-11; Luke 16:19-31

GET STARTED
Lesson 4. Is Hell Really That Bad?

GRAPPLE SCHEDULE

5 MINUTES	HANG TIME
10 MINUTES	GRAPPLE CHAT
10-15 MINUTES	GRAPPLE TIME
20-25 MINUTES	TEAM TIME
10 MINUTES	TEAM REPORTS
5 MINUTES	PRAYER & CHALLENGE

SUPPLIES
Bibles, Grapple DVD, DVD player, music CD, CD player, copy of the Grapple Team Guide for each person, 3x5 cards, pens or pencils, masking tape, garden twine

BIBLE BASIS FOR TEACHERS
The Passages: Luke 16:19-31; Psalm 22:1-11

In the first scene of this parable, Jesus describes the rich man as being splendidly clothed in purple and fine linen and living each day in luxury. During the time of Jesus' earthly ministry, wealthy individuals protected their property with walls and with guards at the gates. Poor and hungry people would sit outside these gates and hope for handouts as the owners and wealthy guests passed through the gates. Jesus describes Lazarus as one of these beggars. It is apparent by the way Jesus tells the story that, throughout his life, the rich man neglected to show compassion for Lazarus and was never moved to help or care for the beggar, even when dogs would lick his open sores.

In the afterlife, the roles were reversed: Lazarus was comforted, and the rich man was tormented. The rich man was suffering the consequences of his lack of compassion, but he was also experiencing the price of not obeying God or Scripture. The punishment was a chasm separating the rich man from the comforts of heaven; no one could cross the chasm in either direction. The rich man hoped that by sending Lazarus back from the dead, Abraham would warn his brothers to change their ways. Abraham told him that if they wouldn't listen to Moses and the prophets, they wouldn't listen to anyone—not even someone who rose from the dead.

How does this relate to the Grapple Question? "See you in hell." This is a common quote in movies and television today. Hell isn't always depicted as a horrible place. In fact, if everyone is going there, hell just seems like a place where the party can continue. For the most part, people outside the church either deny the existence of hell or don't perceive it as being that bad. Through the study of the parable of the rich man and Lazarus, students will grapple with what the world would be like without love, peace, kindness, and joy. Students will discuss what life would be like without God and all the great blessings that God brings to this life and the next.

How does this connect to Jesus? When Jesus was on the cross, he yelled out the first verse of the Psalm 22: "My God, my God, why have you abandoned me?" As we finish reading Psalm 22, we realize that God didn't abandon Jesus during his greatest need but, instead, brought victory through this painful experience. Nevertheless, Jesus truly experienced hell while dying on the cross. Although God did not abandon Jesus, Jesus felt as if God was nowhere to be found. Jesus experienced hell so that we would never have to experience it ourselves. That's great news! Because of Jesus we don't ever have to experience life completely separated from God.

GRAPPLE HANG TIME: 5 MINUTES
Play music as kids enjoy snacks and friendship; then play an opening countdown from the Grapple DVD to wrap up Grapple Hang Time.

GRAPPLE CHAT
Have students form pairs; if you have an uneven number of kids, it's OK to have one trio in the mix. Ask each group to chat about two of the four topics below that relate to today's grapple topic. (Answers in parentheses are samples.)

IN PAIRS
Chat 1: List at least three people in the Bible who got into big trouble with God. (Lot's wife, Genesis 19:26; the man of God, 1 Kings 13:20-22; Moses and Aaron, Numbers 20:12)

Chat 2: Do you believe you will live to be at least 100 years old? Why or why not? Have any of your relatives lived that long?

Chat 3: Find a verse that shows someone with a physical limitation. (Samson, Judges 16:21; the lame man, Acts 14:8)

Chat 4: Think about the worst sunburn you've ever had. How bad was it, and how long did it last?

GRAPPLE TIME: 10-15 MINUTES
Get Ready: Cue the Grapple DVD to the "Life by the Numbers" clip. Stick a strip of masking tape across the middle of the floor, and cut the twine into 3-foot lengths.

Hand each person a 3x5 card and a pen or pencil, and lead the entire class in the following:

Pair up with someone and choose one partner to "tell" and the other person to "guess." I'm going to ask you a list of questions that your partner who is "telling" will answer by writing the answers on the card. The partner who is "guessing" will also write an answer on a card, trying to guess what the other partner has written. You want the answers on your cards to match—but you cannot say or communicate anything to each other as you're answering these questions.

Give everyone time to get in pairs, and then read aloud the following questions (or replace with questions that might be a better fit for your group):

- What is your favorite pizza topping?
- What was the best Christmas gift you ever received?
- What country would you most like to visit?
- What is the first movie you ever saw in a theater?
- What is your favorite sport to play?

When students finish writing answers, have them line up on the strip of tape with partners facing each other, and hand each pair a piece of twine.

Now we're going to see just how long you can stay connected to your partner. I'm going to repeat the questions one by one so you can read your answers to each other. If the answers don't match, then one of you takes a step backward. Try to hold on to the twine as long as you can, but if you have to let go, you must start over again.

Read the questions back through in the same order, as pairs read the answers on their cards.

IN PAIRS
How did it feel the moment that you were forced to let go of the twine and be "cut off" from your partner? When have you felt cut off from your friends or family? When have you felt cut off from God? According to Scripture, love is one of the defining qualities of God. What is your most defining quality? Write it down on the other side of your card.

TELL ALL
What did you write? Have you based that quality on your idea of yourself or on the feedback you get from others? Explain. Imagine that, suddenly, everything good in your life was gone. How would your defining quality change?

Let's watch a video to learn more about this.

Show the "Life by the Numbers" clip on the Grapple DVD.

It's easy to think of hell as a place of pain and suffering, because that's what we've probably been taught. But is hell really a place to go and burn forever, or is the emotional separation from God worse than a life of physical flames? Let's grapple with that!

GRAPPLE TEAM TIME: 20-25 MINUTES

Break into Grapple Teams. Encourage Grapple Team leaders to check in with kids about their week. Grapple Team leaders will facilitate discussion, using the Grapple Team Guide on pages 41-42. Afterward, students will report what they learned.

GRAPPLE TEAM REPORTS: 10 MINUTES

At the end of Grapple Team Time, match Grapple Teams that chose Option 1 with Grapple Teams that chose Option 2 from page 42. Have teams present their reports. (If you have an uneven number of teams, simply form one group of three teams for the presentations. If you have only two Grapple Teams, simply do the presentations one team at a time.)

GRAPPLE PRAYER AND CHALLENGE: 5 MINUTES

Read the Grapple Prayer options. Have the class choose one prayer option that everyone will do. Allow students time to pray about what they discovered. Then close in prayer.

Option 1: Prayer Partners

Find a partner to pray with. Talk about troubles you currently face, especially anything connected to today's lesson. Then pray for each other to be able to see your situation from God's perspective.

Option 2: Strong Foundation

Stand up, and close your eyes. While balancing on one foot, silently ask God to help you with a challenging situation you're facing right now. Stay in this position as long as you can—up to two minutes, if possible. Then stand on two feet and ask God to help you be a person who will stand confidently in God's strength.

GRAPPLE CHALLENGE

Sure, Hollywood makes it seem as if sinners have all the fun and that hell may be nothing more than the party that never sleeps. But when the Israelites continued to disobey God and pursue their own selfish desires, they were sent into exile: a place of separation from their land and from their meeting place with God. To them, this fate was worse than death! Hell is the worst form of exile, the worst kind of torment.

This week, instead of pretending hell does not exist or imagining it as a fun place to party, embrace heaven and hell as choices—one that joins us with God forever, and one that separates us from God forever. I encourage you to accept the gift of life we have been given through Jesus. You know about it; now live it and share it!

WEEKLY GRAPPLE CONNECTION
Grapple Question: Is Hell Really That Bad?
Kids Learn: Hell Is Separation From God
Dig Into the Bible: Luke 16:19-31

TV and movies talk about hell casually, as if it's not that bad to be there. We can sometimes forget what makes hell so horrible—being separated from God forever. What would be hard for your family to give up forever? Video games? Desserts? Laser tag? Challenge family members to do without something they like, just for a week. Remind each other that hell means a permanent separation from what we love and need most—God's love and goodness.

- -

GRAPPLE TEAM GUIDE

GRAPPLE TEAM GUIDE LESSON 4

In your Grapple Team, use this guide to grapple with today's question.

According to Guinness World Records, a Texan named Jackie Bibby set a very bizarre record in 2007. Bibby sat in a bathtub for 45 minutes, which is nothing incredible by itself. But when you consider that there were 87 rattlesnakes in the tub with him, it was no picnic. On a separate sheet of paper, make a list of 10 things you could do for 24 hours without stopping, and make a list of the top 10 things you would never try.

IN PAIRS

Why is it difficult to imagine the concept of "eternity"? Picture yourself spending eternity doing only the things you listed as "never try." How do you feel about that? Was there ever a time in your life when you thought you were "going through hell"? If so, explain what made it like hell.

Read Exodus 34:6

Here in this dialogue with Moses, God calls himself compassionate, merciful, slow to anger, loving, and faithful. Rank these attributes from 1 to 5, putting "1" beside the characteristic of God for which you are most thankful.

____ Compassionate ____ Merciful ____ Slow to Anger ____ Loving ____ Faithful

IN PAIRS

How have you seen evidence of God's "unfailing love and faithfulness" in your life recently? If God feels this way about all his creations, then what does God feel about those who will be separated from him for eternity?

Read Psalm 22:1-11

In this psalm, David describes what it's like to feel separated from God. In your Grapple Team, describe a time you felt separated from God. What was it about this experience that you found to be the most distressing?

Read Luke 16:19-31

Imagine you're putting on a theater production of "The Rich Man and Lazarus." Write out a description of the characters and a brief plot summary, including your best guess as to how it all will end.

The Rich Man: _____.

Lazarus: _____.

Abraham: _____.

The Five Brothers: _____.

Plot Summary: _____

_____.

How did the choices of the two main characters affect their conditions after death? Can a person escape from hell or communicate with the living while in hell? Why or why not? What does this passage say about the eternal destination of your friends and family?

GRAPPLE TEAM REPORTS

With your team, choose one of the options below to report what you discovered.

Option 1: Proverb It

Look through the book of Proverbs and find one verse that best connects to what you learned today. If you have enough time, consider finding additional verses.

Option 2: Top 5

Create a Top 5 list of the most important, challenging, or meaningful things you learned today. Be prepared to explain why each item on the list is so important, challenging, or meaningful.

IS HELL REALLY THAT BAD?

Revelation 4:8b
"Holy, holy, holy is the Lord God, the Almighty—the one who always was, who is, and who is still to come."

GRAPPLE CHAT

Chat 1: List at least three people in the Bible who got into big trouble with God.

Chat 2: Do you believe you will live to be at least 100 years old? Why or why not? Have any of your relatives lived that long?

Chat 3: Find a verse that shows someone with a physical limitation.

Chat 4: Think about the worst sunburn you've ever had. How bad was it, and how long did it last?

GRAPPLE CHALLENGE

Spend some time this week trying to describe the worst possible experience, and then consider the idea that hell is worse than anything you can comprehend.

NOTES:

_____

_____

_____

_____

_____

_____

_____

DO-OVERS

WHAT IF I REALLY MESS UP?

DO-OVERS

What if I Really Mess Up?
The Point: Jesus Died for Me
The Passages: 2 Samuel 12:1-14; John 21:15-19

GET STARTED
Lesson 5. What if I Really Mess Up?

GRAPPLE SCHEDULE

5 MINUTES	HANG TIME
10 MINUTES	GRAPPLE CHAT
10-15 MINUTES	GRAPPLE TIME
20-25 MINUTES	TEAM TIME
10 MINUTES	TEAM REPORTS
5 MINUTES	PRAYER & CHALLENGE

SUPPLIES
Bibles, Grapple DVD, DVD player, music CD, CD player, copy of the Grapple Team Guide for each person, 3x5 cards, pens or pencils

BIBLE BASIS FOR TEACHERS
The Passage: 2 Samuel 12:1-14
Although Nathan was a prophet, he showed tremendous courage when he confronted David about his sin. David had already killed once to cover up his sin with Bathsheba. What was to stop him from killing again to cover up the sin of killing Uriah? In spite of that possibility, Nathan did what God sent him to do.

Nathan told David a story about a rich man who stole and ate a poor man's only lamb instead of preparing one of his own lambs. The rich man had flocks of sheep, and the poor man treated his lamb like one of his children. After hearing this story, David was furious. He said that anyone who would do such a thing deserved to die. Nathan then told David that he was the rich man in the story.

David was stricken with guilt. He confessed his sin to God, and God forgave him. David's sin had consequences; David was definitely punished. Nevertheless, the Bible refers to David as a man after God's own heart (see 1 Samuel 13:13-14; Acts 13:22). David wrote eloquently of his remorse and repentance in Psalm 51. David's sin devastated him and his kingdom, but he sought forgiveness in one of the most beautiful psalms of contrition ever written. His plea for cleansing is an example for us all, who, like David, are sinners.

How does this relate to the Grapple Question? David really messed up. He desired a married woman, lured her into committing adultery with him, and

47

then tried to cover it up. When his attempts to cover up his mistakes failed, he murdered her husband in order to fix his situation once and for all. In fact, he didn't confess his sin until he was confronted by a prophet of God. Yet David asked for forgiveness, and it was granted. Like David, we all sin. And like David, we receive God's forgiveness when we ask for it. Even so, David had to face the music, and so do we; there are still consequences for our actions.

How does this connect to Jesus? God loves us and wants to be in relationship with us. When we sin, our relationship with God suffers. When we confess and ask for forgiveness, that friendship with God is rekindled. By dying on the cross and coming back to life, Jesus made this process possible. Jesus separates us from our sins, and faith in him connects us directly to God. Our actions will have consequences, but the ultimate consequence—eternal separation from God—was removed from the equation by Jesus Christ.

GRAPPLE HANG TIME: 5 MINUTES
Play music as kids enjoy snacks and friendship, and then play an opening countdown from the Grapple DVD.

GRAPPLE CHAT
Have students form pairs; if you have an uneven number of kids, it's OK to have one trio in the mix. Ask each group to chat about two of the four topics below that relate to today's grapple topic. (Answers in parentheses are samples.)

IN PAIRS
Chat 1: Find three examples in the Bible of someone forgiving someone else. (Esau forgave Jacob; Joseph forgave his brothers; Jesus forgave the paralyzed man.)

Chat 2: When did you most recently forgive another person, and how did it feel to offer forgiveness?

Chat 3: How many times did Jesus tell Peter he needed to forgive someone? (Seventy times seven or seventy-seven times, depending on the translation)

Chat 4: What's the most recent gift you receive, and what did you appreciate most about it?

GRAPPLE TIME: 10-15 MINUTES
Get Ready: Cue the Grapple DVD to the "Drive-Through Windows" clip.

Lead the entire class in the following:

Today we're going to play a game of Simon Says. Here's the twist. The first time you miss, you can stay in the game, but you have to close your eyes. The second time you miss, you can stay in the game, but you have to also close your ears with your fingers so you can't see or hear. Keep playing until you miss a third time—and then you're out.

Play the game for a couple of minutes; it doesn't matter how many are left in the game at that time.

Here's a refresher on how to play Simon Says: Tell your students to do actions such as "stand up," "sit down," "spin around," "raise your hand," or anything you can think of. Whenever your instruction includes "Simon says," kids should do exactly what you say. If you don't say "Simon says," students should not do what you say. If kids mess up once, they get the first consequence. If they mess up a second time, they add the second consequence. If they mess up a third time, they're out of the game. The idea is to do this as quickly as you can and try to get students to obey instructions that don't include "Simon says."

TELL ALL
How did the consequences for messing up affect your ability to play the game? If you kept playing with one or more consequences, did you feel like giving up? Why or why not?

IN PAIRS
Think of a time you experienced a consequence for a mistake. What effect did the consequence have on you? Which is better—to experience a consequence for a mistake or a poor choice, or to be given a second chance with no consequence at all? Explain.

TELL ALL
What did you talk about?

Let's watch a video to see how we sometimes see God's forgiveness as the "easy button" way out of the consequences of our sins.

Show the "Drive-Through Windows" clip on the Grapple DVD.

Do we have a basic right to be forgiven by God for the things we do? What if you really mess up? Can God forgive everything? And what does God's forgiveness look like? Let's grapple with that.

GRAPPLE TEAM TIME: 20-25 MINUTES
Break into Grapple Teams. Encourage Grapple Team leaders to check in with kids about their week. Grapple Team leaders will facilitate discussion, using the Grapple Team Guide on page 51. Afterward, students will report what they learned.

GRAPPLE TEAM REPORTS: 10 MINUTES

At the end of Grapple Team Time, match Grapple Teams that chose Option 1 with Grapple Teams that chose Option 2 from pages 51-52. Have teams present their reports.

(If you have an uneven number of teams, simply form one group of three teams for the presentations. If you have only two Grapple Teams, simply do the presentations one team at a time.)

GRAPPLE PRAYER AND CHALLENGE: 5 MINUTES

Read the Grapple Prayer options. Have the class choose one prayer option that everyone will do. Allow students some time to pray about what they wrote on their cards and what they discovered today. Then close in prayer.

Option 1: Psalms That Pray

Get comfortable, preferably sitting apart from each other. Look through the book of Psalms and find a psalm that connects with a situation you're facing right now. Read the psalm quietly as a prayer to God.

Option 2: Power Prayers

Clench your fists tight as you imagine using all your power to maintain control over all the different areas of your life. Talk with God, asking for his powerful perspective, and gradually unclench your fists as you give God control. With your hands open and empty, ask God to fill you with his empowering, life-giving Spirit.

GRAPPLE CHALLENGE

David was known as a man after God's own heart. Peter was one of Jesus' closest friends and disciples. But even David and Peter messed up. No one is perfect, and everyone sins. The good news is that God will forgive us and will forget all about our sins. God loves us and wants to be friends with us. God also wants us to love other people. I challenge you to forgive someone who has hurt you in the past—or to ask for forgiveness from someone you have hurt.

WEEKLY GRAPPLE CONNECTION
Grapple Question: What if I Really Mess Up?
Kids Learn: Jesus Died for Them
Dig Into the Bible: 2 Samuel 12:1-14; John 21:15-19

Everyone sins. It's a fact of life. Sometimes, though, teenagers think they've really done it—so much so that they come to the conclusion that even God couldn't forgive them for their latest, greatest sin. This week guide your child into understanding that God is ready to forgive us for anything we do. Share a time in your life when you really messed up, and talk about how you are assured that God has forgiven you. Help your teenager realize that Jesus died for the sins of everyone, no matter how severe we might think our sins are.

GRAPPLE TEAM GUIDE LESSON 5

In your Grapple Team, use this guide to grapple with today's question.

Read 2 Samuel 12:1-14

Keep in mind that David lusted after a married woman named Bathsheba and made sure her husband got killed in battle to cover his sin. Then the prophet Nathan came to see David. He told David a story about a rich man who took a poor man's only sheep and killed it to serve to a guest. David was furious with the rich man in the story.

IN PAIRS

Were the consequences David received for his sin fair? Why or why not? If you had to live under those consequences, what would you be feeling? What difference does being forgiven make if you still have to experience consequences for your sin? If you had been David, would you have used "the easy button"? Why or why not?

Now read about a conversation between Jesus and Peter. It happened after Jesus came back to life but before he left his disciples. Remember, Peter betrayed Jesus by denying he even knew him three times while Jesus was being condemned to death. As far as we know, this is the first one-to-one conversation Jesus and Peter have had since Peter's betrayal.

Read John 21:15-19

IN PAIRS

What "consequences" had Peter experienced for his betrayal of Jesus, if any? If you had been Peter, how would you have felt during this conversation? What do you think Jesus was trying to do in this conversation? Take your best shot—what impact do you think this encounter had on Peter?

GRAPPLE TEAM REPORTS

With your team, choose one of the options below to report what you discovered.

Option 1: Dialogue

Create a scene from your everyday life that includes dialogue involving everyone on your team (or several sample conversations) to demonstrate what you've learned today.

Option 2: Text It
Write a 140-character text message that you could send to a friend or family member explaining what you learned today.

WHAT IF I REALLY MESS UP?

Ephesians 2:8-9
God saved you by his grace when you believed. And you can't take credit for this; it is a gift from God. Salvation is not a reward for the good things we have done, so none of us can boast about it.

GRAPPLE CHAT

Chat 1: Find three examples in the Bible of someone forgiving someone else.

Chat 2: When did you most recently forgive another person, and how did it feel to offer forgiveness?

Chat 3: How many times did Jesus tell Peter he needed to forgive someone?

Chat 4: What's the most recent gift you receive, and what did you appreciate most about it?

GRAPPLE CHALLENGE

Forgive someone this week, or ask for forgiveness from someone else.

NOTES:

_____

_____

_____

_____

_____

_____

_____

_____

DO-OVERS

DON'T ALL GOOD PEOPLE GO TO HEAVEN?

DO-OVERS

Don't All Good People Go to Heaven?
The Point: Jesus Is My Only Hope
The Passages: Matthew 7:24-27; Mark 10:17-27; Ephesians 2:8-9

GET STARTED
Lesson 6. Don't All Good People Go to Heaven?

GRAPPLE SCHEDULE

5 MINUTES	HANG TIME
10 MINUTES	GRAPPLE CHAT
10-15 MINUTES	GRAPPLE TIME
20-25 MINUTES	TEAM TIME
10 MINUTES	TEAM REPORTS
5 MINUTES	PRAYER & CHALLENGE

SUPPLIES
Bibles, Grapple DVD, DVD player, music CD, CD player, copy of the Grapple Team Guide for each person, paper, pens or pencils, plastic construction blocks (or wooden blocks), rubber bands, copies of maps printed from a mapping website

BIBLE BASIS FOR TEACHERS
The Passage: Mark 10:17-27

This man who ran up to Jesus might have thought he had it all figured out. He tried to do the right thing and be a good person. When he asked Jesus what he needed to do to inherit eternal life, he may have thought he knew the answer. Jesus responded by reminding the man of the commandments. The man knew them and obeyed them. Jesus felt "genuine love" for this man, but he saw that another master held the man back. Jesus isn't saying that obeying the commandments, selling all of your property, and giving to the needy ensure a straight ticket into heaven. Jesus is pointing out a significant roadblock in this man's devotion to God.

After hearing Jesus' message, the man went away sad. He didn't do what Jesus asked him to do. When Jesus told others to drop what they were doing and follow him, most of them did. This man recognized that his wealth was more important to him than his desire to follow Christ, and that was a problem if he wanted to inherit eternal life. Jesus says "it is easier for a camel to go through the eye of a needle than for a rich person to enter the Kingdom of God!" It is not possible for a camel to go through the eye of a needle, as the disciples recognized. Achieving eternal life by obeying commandments or doing good deeds—in other words, through human means—is also impossible. However, everything is possible with God.

How does this relate to the Grapple Question? It's interesting that Jesus' first response to this well-to-do individual was a question: "Why do you call me good?" Right off the bat being good is thrown out on the table. Can you go to heaven by being a good person? No. It's about as possible as a camel walking through the eye of a needle. This rich man was the best person around, but he wasn't able to make Jesus his Lord. He had other things that were more important to him than Jesus, and those things got in the way.

How does this connect to Jesus? Without Jesus, we have no hope of having eternal life. We can do good things, but they'll never add up to enough. It would be easier to stuff a 2,000-pound camel through the eye of a needle than to earn your way into heaven. The good news is you don't have to earn it. Jesus said that with God anything is possible. By dying and coming back to life, Jesus made the impossible possible. Faith in Jesus is the way to heaven, and that's a lot easier than stuffing camels through teeny, tiny holes.

GRAPPLE HANG TIME: 5 MINUTES
Play music as kids enjoy snacks and friendship, and then play an opening countdown from the Grapple DVD to wrap up Grapple Hang Time.

GRAPPLE CHAT
Have students form pairs; if you have an uneven number of kids, it's OK to have one trio in the mix. Ask each group to chat about two of the four topics below that relate to today's grapple topic. (Answers in parentheses are samples.)

IN PAIRS
Chat 1: According to the Bible, what was the first skyscraper? (Tower of Babel, Genesis 11)

Chat 2: When you get older, would you ever want to be a builder or an architect? Why or why not?

Chat 3: Find a Bible verse or passage that says we receive salvation through God's grace and not by doing good things. (Ephesians 2:8-9)

Chat 4: Have you ever won a "perfect attendance" award? If not, what's the longest streak you've been at school without a sick day?

GRAPPLE TIME: 10-15 MINUTES
Get Ready: Cue the Grapple DVD to "All Dogs Go to Heaven."

Lead the entire class in the following:

Have kids get into four teams.

This game is called Tower Time. I'll give each team approximately the same amount of plastic construction blocks (or wooden blocks). You have five minutes to construct a tower. The goal is to make it as high and indestructible as possible. After construction, the opposing teams will have a chance to knock down your tower with rubber bands.

Have all four teams begin construction. After five minutes, tell students to stop immediately.

Here's the catch: Each member of the team with the highest tower gets three rubber bands and gets to shoot from 8 inches away. Students on the team with the second highest tower get two rubber bands each and can shoot from 12 inches away. People on the third team get one rubber band each and can shoot from 16 inches away. Members of the fourth team only get one rubber band each and have to shoot from 20 inches away.

Hand out rubber bands to students on each team according to the instructions.

Begin firing on my count, and then we'll see if any of the towers remain. Three, two, one, FIRE!

IN PAIRS
What lessons did you learn about tower building from this competition? If you could go back in time and give your team the best advice for this competition, what would it be? How might your advice apply to our relationship with God?

Read Matthew 7:24-27

What do you think it means to build your life on a rock?

Let's watch a DVD clip as we think more about what it truly takes to inherit eternal life.

Show "All Dogs Go to Heaven" on the Grapple DVD.

Everyone would like to think that all dogs go to heaven, and maybe they do. We feel the same way about people. Sometimes it feels selfish and conceited to think that Christianity is the only way. Why would God not let good people go to heaven, just because they don't believe in Jesus? Can't we just live good lives and earn a spot in heaven? Let's grapple with that.

GRAPPLE TEAM TIME: 20-25 MINUTES
Break into Grapple Teams. Encourage Grapple Team leaders to check in with kids about their week. Grapple Team leaders will facilitate discussion, using the Grapple Team Guide on pages 61-62. Afterward, students will report what they learned.

GRAPPLE TEAM REPORTS: 10 MINUTES

At the end of Grapple Team Time, match Grapple Teams that chose Option 1 with Grapple Teams that chose Option 2 from pages 62-63. Have teams present their reports. (If you have an uneven number of teams, simply form one group of three teams for the presentations. If you have only two Grapple Teams, simply do the presentations one team at a time.)

GRAPPLE PRAYER AND CHALLENGE: 5 MINUTES

Read the Grapple Prayer options. Have the class choose one prayer option that everyone will do. Allow students time to pray about what they discovered. Then close in prayer.

Get Ready

For Option 1, make sure students have paper and pens or pencils. For Option 2, distribute copies of maps printed from a mapping website.

Option 1: Prayer Pile

Get in a circle with the rest of your group. Write a prayer to God. Then crumple up the paper with the prayer on it and make a pile of crumpled papers in the middle of the circle. Choose one crumpled prayer from the pile. Silently pray the words written on the paper, and then ask God to answer the prayer for the person who wrote it.

Option 2: Roadmap of Wisdom

Look at a map, and consider all the different roads and highways and streets feature on that map. Pray for God's guidance, wisdom, and direction in your life, and ask God for strength in following the path and plan he has created for you.

GRAPPLE CHALLENGE

A friend of mine told me once, "What you have, has you." It's time to let go and trust God with everything. We can do good things, but they'll never add up to enough to earn salvation and eternity in heaven. This next week, every time you feel like you're holding on to something that is becoming a distraction or is an attempt to make yourself more deserving of God's love, whisper to yourself "I'm letting go and trusting you, God." And in that moment, release whatever it is.

WEEKLY GRAPPLE CONNECTION

Grapple Question: Don't All Good People Go to Heaven?
Kids Learn: Jesus Is Their Only Hope
Dig Into the Bible: Mark 10:17-27; Ephesians 2:8-9

You hear it all the time: "If there is a heaven, I'm pretty sure I'll get in. I'm a good person; God wouldn't send me to hell." Young adolescents are beginning to struggle with this issue on a regular basis. Often times, kids conclude that heaven is a reward for good behavior. They see God as a teacher awarding A's for superb performance, and heaven is the dessert for eating their vegetables. This week try letting everyone eat dessert before the meal in order to illustrate God's gift of salvation. Finish your meal by reading Ephesians 2:8-9 to help your kids see heaven as a gift rather than a reward. Tell them that eternal life is a free gift if they believe in Jesus; they don't have to do anything else.

- -

GRAPPLE TEAM GUIDE LESSON 6

In your Grapple Team, use this guide to grapple with today's question.

Before you look at one of the many surprising—and very important—questions that Jesus was asked, it's time for a gut check.

List things (other than food and water) that you can't live without. (For instance, maybe you can't live without your guitar.)

_____

_____

IN PAIRS

Share your answers. Then discuss the following list. Which are things that you cannot possibly live without? Write "Yes" if you think you must have it or "No" if you could survive without it.

Money: _____
Admiration from others: _____
Sports: _____
Girlfriend/boyfriend: _____
Best friend: _____
Lots of friends: _____
Dream job: _____
Good health: _____
Happiness: _____

Read Mark 10:17-27

Circle the three words that best describe the man who ran up to Jesus:
proud, humble, kind, loveable, strong, cool, dorky, nerdy, good, bad, likeable, friendly, showoff, cocky, selfish, intense, shallow, curious

Why did you choose those words? Who do you know that reminds you of this man? Why?

_____

_____

Verse 21 says that Jesus felt genuine love for the man. How could knowing how Jesus felt about the rich man help you when sharing with others about Jesus being the only way to God?

_____

_____

IN PAIRS

Jesus asks a lot of this guy. Discuss whether you think Jesus was fair to him. What about you? What if Jesus turned to you and told you to sell all your possessions, to give up everything that holds value to you, to let go of reaching or achieving all of your desires and dreams, and follow him? Do you think you could do it? Why or why not?

If we're honest, we would be like the disciples and say that, if getting eternal life takes giving Jesus everything, it really is impossible. Jesus even says it's easier for a camel to go through the eye of a needle than for a rich person to enter the kingdom of God! Does this mean rich people can't ever get into heaven? Why or why not? How is it possible for anyone to get into heaven?

Read Ephesians 2:8-9

Why is it good that we can't take credit for our salvation and that we can't earn salvation through the good things we do? How is this good news for us?

_____

_____

GRAPPLE TEAM REPORTS

With your team, choose one of the options below to report what you discovered.

Get Ready
For Option 2, make sure students have paper and pens or pencils.

Option 1: Movie Illustration
Together, think of a scene from a movie that illustrates what you learned today. Be prepared to describe that scene and explain why it illustrates what you've learned.

Option 2: Preach It; Practice It
Create a short instruction manual titled "Practice What You Preach." Come up with at least 10 ways everyone can put today's lesson into practice this next week.

DON'T ALL GOOD PEOPLE GO TO HEAVEN?

Ephesians 2:8-9
God saved you by his grace when you believed. And you can't take credit for this; it is a gift from God. Salvation is not a reward for the good things we have done, so none of us can boast about it.

GRAPPLE CHAT

Chat 1: According to the Bible, what was the first skyscraper?

Chat 2: When you get older, would you ever want to be a builder or an architect? Why or why not?

Chat 3: Find a Bible verse or passage that says we receive salvation through God's grace and not by doing good things.

Chat 4: Have you ever won a "perfect attendance" award? If not, what's the longest streak you've been at school without a sick day?

GRAPPLE CHALLENGE

This week, look for ways to put God first—above everything else in your life.

NOTES:

_____

_____

_____

_____

_____

_____

_____

DO-OVERS

CAN I DO ANYTHING
I WANT?

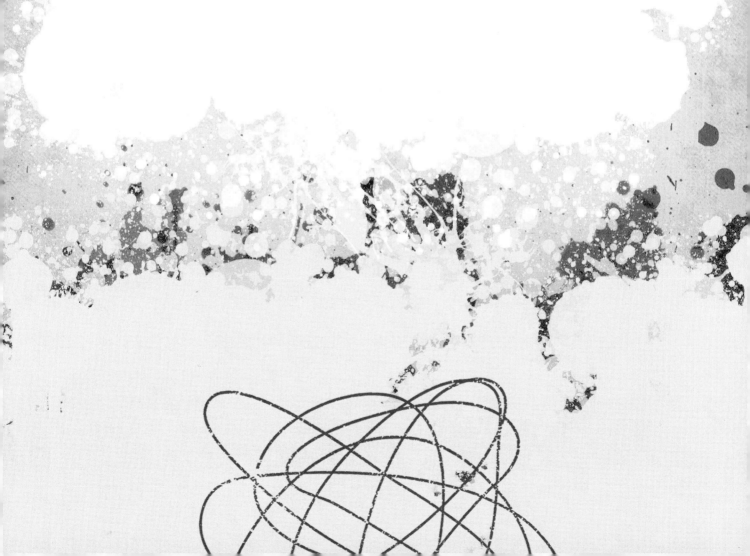

DO-OVERS

Can I Do Anything I Want?
The Point: I Want to Honor Jesus
The Passages: John 8:1-11; Romans 6:15-18

GET STARTED
Lesson 7. Can I Do Anything I Want?

GRAPPLE SCHEDULE

5 MINUTES	HANG TIME
10 MINUTES	GRAPPLE CHAT
10-15 MINUTES	GRAPPLE TIME
20-25 MINUTES	TEAM TIME
10 MINUTES	TEAM REPORTS
5 MINUTES	PRAYER & CHALLENGE

SUPPLIES
Bibles, Grapple DVD, DVD player, music CD, CD player, copy of the Grapple Team Guide for each person, paper, pens or pencils, chalk, markers (if doing Grapple Time activity indoors), bull's-eye

BIBLE BASIS FOR TEACHERS
The Passage: John 8:1-11

Jesus came to Jerusalem for the Festival of Shelters (or Booths). He taught in the Temple during the day, but because some of the Jews were looking to arrest him, he retreated at night to the Mount of Olives. Every morning, however, Jesus returned to the Temple to continue teaching the people. On this particular day, the Pharisees wanted to trap Jesus into saying something that they could use against him.

When they approached Jesus, they brought with them a woman who had been caught in the act of adultery. According to Jewish law, if a man commits adultery with another man's wife, both the man and the woman are to be put to death (see Leviticus 20:10). It's interesting that the woman was the only participant brought before Jesus. Where was the man? Why wasn't he also one of the accused? Jesus recognized that the man was missing. He was also aware that the Pharisees were trying to trap him. The Pharisees knew that Jesus consistently stood up for sinners and other marginalized individuals. They hoped that Jesus would protect this woman and, in doing so, go against the Law of Moses. Instead, Jesus turned the table on the Pharisees. Suddenly, the accusers become the accused. Only those who were without sin could cast judgment. When the accusers withdrew, Jesus assured the woman that no one condemned her, and he told her not to sin anymore.

How does this relate to the Grapple Question? Grace is a wonderful gift that often gets misconstrued. "If God will forgive me anyway, why can't I do whatever I want?" Some people are under the impression that people who sin and disobey God are fun and people who obey God are fun-haters. "Why not have fun, hang out with fun people, and live the life we want to live? God will forgive us anyway; no one will condemn us because everyone sins." Jesus specifically commanded the adulterous woman to sin no more. She was offered the gift of grace and forgiveness first, and then she responded to that grace by living righteously. No one's perfect, but we are to respond to God's gifts with an appreciative and obedient heart.

How does this connect to Jesus? Jesus' sacrifice on the cross and his victory over death through his resurrection provide the gift of forgiveness and eternal life with God in heaven. God no longer condemns us. Because of Christ, the Holy Spirit transforms our lives and empowers us to flee from sin. Doing good works will not get us into the kingdom of God, but because we are part of the kingdom of God, we do good works.

GRAPPLE HANG TIME: 5 MINUTES
Play music as kids enjoy snacks and friendship, and then play an opening countdown from the Grapple DVD to wrap up Grapple Hang Time.

GRAPPLE CHAT
Have students form pairs; if you have an uneven number of kids, it's OK to have one trio in the mix. Ask each group to chat about two of the four topics below that relate to today's grapple topic. (Answers in parentheses are samples.)

IN PAIRS
Chat 1: Find three different ways a rock or stone is used in the Bible. (Jacob used a stone as a pillow at Bethel; David used five smooth stones to kill Goliath; a great stone was rolled in front of Jesus' tomb.)

Chat 2: What was your most embarrassing moment in the past week? How did it compare to the most embarrassing experience ever in your life?

Chat 3: Everyone sins—even people in the Bible. Find five people in the Bible, and identify one sin each person committed. (Jacob: lying; Moses: murder; Aaron: idolatry; David: adultery; Paul: hatred)

Chat 4: How long until you're old enough to drive? What do you think that experience will be like?

GRAPPLE TIME: 10-15 MINUTES
Get Ready: Cue the Grapple DVD to "Some Friend."

Lead the entire class in the following:

Let's go outside and draw pictures on the sidewalk of things that make us happy. Then we'll each explain why we drew our particular pictures.

Take everyone to the parking lot, and give each person chalk. (If it is too cold or wet—or if you don't have permission to draw on the sidewalk outside your meeting area—stay indoors, and give each person paper and markers.)

IN PAIRS

Imagine that instead of depicting what makes you happy, you were asked to draw the very worst thing you've ever done and then share it with everyone. What would you do? Why?

TELL ALL

Share your answers with the group. Now imagine that because of Jesus, the chalk suddenly becomes invisible. No one can see what you've done in the past and no one will ever be able to see what you do in the future. Now how do you feel about what you've done? How do you feel about things you are tempted to do in the future? Why?

Let's watch a DVD clip as we think more about forgiveness.

Show the "Some Friend" clip on the Grapple DVD.

Today, we're going to read about a woman who had the worst things from her life put on display before the world and how Jesus made it all go away. If Jesus forgives us for everything we've done and everything we will do, can't we do whatever we want to do? Let's grapple with that.

GRAPPLE TEAM TIME: 20-25 MINUTES

Break into Grapple Teams. Encourage Grapple Team leaders to check in with kids about their week. Grapple Team leaders will facilitate discussion, using the Grapple Team Guide on pages 73-74. Afterward, students will report what they learned.

GRAPPLE TEAM REPORTS: 10 MINUTES

At the end of Grapple Team Time, match Grapple Teams that chose Option 1 with Grapple Teams that chose Option 2 from page 74. Have teams present their reports.

(If you have an uneven number of teams, simply form one group of three teams for the presentations. If you have only two Grapple Teams, simply do the presentations one team at a time.)

GRAPPLE PRAYER AND CHALLENGE: 5 MINUTES

Read the Grapple Prayer options. Have the class choose one prayer option that everyone will do. Allow students time to pray about what they discovered. Then close in prayer.

Get Ready

For Option 2, affix the bull's-eye to the far wall, and distribute paper to students.

Option 1: Little and Big

Think of "little" sins from this past week that you might have thought were too insignificant to confess. Confess these to God, and ask God to help you change your attitude about all sin—even the "little" sins.

Option 2: Marksman, Markswoman

Make paper airplanes, and take turns throwing the airplanes at the bull's-eye. Walk to wherever your airplane lands and pray to God about one way you miss the mark in your life. Relate what you say to what you learned today.

GRAPPLE CHALLENGE

We experience freedom in Christ. However, that freedom is meant for life not death. Thing we think might make life more exciting can leave us battered and broken. Before making your next decision, take a spiritual gut check. Ask yourself, "Will this bring me closer to honoring Jesus, or will it take me further away from Jesus?" If the answer is "closer," go for it! If it is "further," don't!

WEEKLY GRAPPLE CONNECTION
Grapple Question: Can I Do Anything I Want?
Kids Learn: They Want to Honor Jesus
Dig Into the Bible: John 8:1-11; Romans 6:15-18

"If being good doesn't get me into heaven, they why be good?" This question may be the next logical step your kids take. Most teenagers have figured out the American way. "If I want to succeed, I must put forth a solid effort; nothing is free. Doing good works takes effort, and if I've already received the fruits of my labor, then there's no need for further labor." For those who follow Jesus, faith is evident in good works. This week, make an extra effort to be an example to your kids. Remind them that doing good works won't get them into heaven; however, when they do good things for others, people will see that the Holy Spirit lives inside their hearts.

GRAPPLE TEAM GUIDE LESSON 7

In your Grapple Team, use this guide to grapple with today's question.

Are you looking forward to getting your driver's license? Of course you are!

IN PAIRS

Tell your partner about your dream car, and explain why that particular car is special to you. What do you think it would feel like to sit behind the wheel of that car?

Read John 8:1-11

The Pharisees tried to put Jesus in a Catch-22. In your own words, explain what was tricky about the situation.

_____

_____

Draw or write what you think Jesus might have written in the sand.

```



```

After everyone left, Jesus told the woman: "Neither do I [condemn you]. Go and sin no more." When we become followers of Christ, it's like we're given a "Freedom License." We're given all the rights of a card-carrying member: eternal life, forgiveness of sins, meaning and significance. But like a driver's license, it does not give us the right to disobey the law. Disobeying traffic rules would be

very dangerous for everyone involved. A driver's license gives us the privilege to drive and the responsibility to drive safely. Our Freedom License gives us the privilege of life, but Jesus still wants us to be responsible in honoring him and to follow the rules so we can avoid dangerous, destructive paths and patterns. In the box below, draw your very own Freedom License.

Read Romans 6:15-18

What are some reasons to try to live a life that is pleasing to God?

_____

_____

GRAPPLE TEAM REPORTS
With your team, choose one of the options below to report what you discovered.

Option 1: ABCs
Write the ABCs of what you learned today: a statement that starts with an A, a statement that starts with a B, and so on. Try to go as far into the alphabet as you can—even all the way to Z.

Option 2: Relay Report
Discuss some of the big ideas you've learned today. Once you're ready to make your presentation to the other team, line up on one side of the room. Run down to the other end of the room and back. When you return, tell about something you learned today. Then the next person in line runs to the end of the room and back, and reports something else. Continue until everyone has participated.

CAN I DO ANYTHING I WANT?

Ephesians 2:8-9
God saved you by his grace when you believed. And you can't take credit for this; it is a gift from God. Salvation is not a reward for the good things we have done, so none of us can boast about it.

GRAPPLE CHAT
Chat 1: Find three different ways a rock or stone is used in the Bible.

Chat 2: What was your most embarrassing moment in the past week? How did it compare to the most embarrassing experience ever in your life?

Chat 3: Everyone sins—even people in the Bible. Find five people in the Bible, and identify one sin each person committed.

Chat 4: How long until you're old enough to drive? What do you think that experience will be like?

GRAPPLE CHALLENGE
Before making your next decision, ask yourself if the decision will bring you closer to honoring Jesus or take you further away from Jesus. If the answer is "closer," go for it! If the answer is "further," don't!

NOTES:

_____

_____

_____

_____

_____

_____

_____

_____

DO-OVERS

IS GOD A WIMP?

DO-OVERS

Is God a Wimp?
The Point: I Get a Do-Over With Jesus
The Passages: Genesis 2:8-17; 3:1-6, 14-19; Romans 5:18

GET STARTED
Lesson 8. Is God a Wimp?

GRAPPLE SCHEDULE

5 MINUTES	HANG TIME
10 MINUTES	GRAPPLE CHAT
10-15 MINUTES	GRAPPLE TIME
20-25 MINUTES	TEAM TIME
10 MINUTES	TEAM REPORTS
5 MINUTES	PRAYER & CHALLENGE

SUPPLIES
Bibles, Grapple DVD, DVD player, music CD, CD player, CD with opening theme music for trivia competition (optional), copy of the Grapple Team Guide for each person, paper, pens or pencils, trivia questions (included in this lesson), markers, copies of maps printed from a mapping website

BIBLE BASIS FOR TEACHERS
The Passage: Genesis 2:8-17; 3:1-6
How could an all-powerful God allow sin to enter into his perfect creation? God created the world and everything in it, and then God created man. God planted a garden, made fruit trees grow up from the ground, and placed the man—Adam—in the garden. God provided Adam with everything he could possibly need and gave him only one warning. God told him that he could eat of any tree in the garden except the tree of the knowledge of good and evil.

The serpent in Genesis is identified later in Scripture as an embodiment of Satan. Satan's goal is ultimately to destroy our relationship with God. God desires our love, devotion, and worship, and Satan's greatest desire is to take that away from God. After God created the woman, whom Adam named Eve, from Adam's rib, the serpent deceived Eve, and then Adam followed suit. The serpent convinced Adam and Eve that God was lying to them to keep them in their place. The serpent suggested that, by eating the fruit from the tree of the knowledge of good and evil, they would be like God, knowing both good and evil. Adam and Eve couldn't resist that temptation, and they gave in and sinned.

How does this relate to the Grapple Question? Because sin, pain, and suffering are very evident in our world today, many people question God's power. "How

can an all-powerful God allow sin to even exist? If God truly was powerful, he would have created humans without the capability to disobey him and sin." God could have created men and women without the potential to sin. However, a creation without the capacity to disobey would also not have the capacity to obey. Ultimately God would be creating robots he could control rather than human beings with the free will to choose God or not. God's greatest desire is for humanity to love and worship him. You cannot program someone to love. True love and devotion to anyone is a choice that springs forth from one's heart. The freedom to make that choice is a necessary component of what God desires from his creation. The tree of the knowledge of good and evil was God's way of providing humanity with that freedom to choose him or to disobey him. God has the power to control the choices of humanity. However, true love and obedience would never take place if the man and the woman were programmed to obey. Unfortunately, Adam and Eve chose to disobey God and thereby altered the course of humanity. God had to provide human beings with a do-over—a second chance.

How does this connect to Jesus? Jesus is the do-over. God warned Adam that if he ate of the tree of the knowledge of good and evil, he would surely die. Romans 6:23 says that the wages of sin is death, but the free gift of God is eternal life through Christ Jesus our Lord. Humanity was condemned to die, both physically and spiritually, through the sinful act of this first man and woman. Thankfully, God had a plan to overcome that curse. God sent his only Son, Jesus Christ, to suffer and die for us. Through Jesus, we are made righteous and inherit eternal life (see Romans 5:18-21).

GRAPPLE HANG TIME: 5 MINUTES
Play music as kids enjoy snacks and friendship, and then play an opening countdown from the Grapple DVD to wrap up Grapple Hang Time.

GRAPPLE CHAT
Have students form pairs; if you have an uneven number of kids, it's OK to have one trio in the mix. Ask each group to chat about two of the four topics below that relate to today's grapple topic. (Answers in parentheses are samples.)

IN PAIRS
Chat 1: Do we know what kind of fruit Adam and Eve ate in the Garden of Eden? (No; the Bible doesn't specify exactly what it was)

Chat 2: What is your favorite movie that shows someone getting a second chance?

Chat 3: Find a verse in the Bible that describes God as the God of second chances. (Exodus 32:14; Jonah 3:10; Jeremiah 26:19)

Chat 4: What do you think it would be like to travel to a country in another part of the world? If you've made such a trip, what was it like?

GRAPPLE TIME: 10-15 MINUTES

Get Ready: Cue the Grapple DVD to "Who's a Wimp?"

Question: Which of the following is NOT an actual name of celebrity children: Suri, Apple, Shiloh, or Vanilla? (Vanilla)

Consequence: Hop on one foot, and touch your nose with your right and left index fingers alternately while reciting the Pledge of Allegiance.

Question: What is the standard size of the numbers of an NFL field? (6x4 feet)

Consequence: Spin in place 10 times and run around the room.

Question: What is the birth name of the blockbuster film star Tom Cruise? (Thomas Mapother IV)

Consequence: Sing "Row, Row, Row Your Boat" in a round.

Question: What is the only U.S. state to form by seceding from a Confederate state? (West Virginia)

Consequence: Perform your best rendition of a scene (preferably a song) from High School Musical.

Question: When ordering pizza, people who have wind chimes on the porch are four times more likely to order what topping? (Olives)

Consequence: Do the Hokey Pokey and turn yourself around because that's what it's all about.

Question: How many minutes does it take the average person to fall asleep? (7)

Consequence: Do 20 jumping jacks while saying the alphabet backward.

NOTE: You're welcome to replace these questions with ones that might be a better fit for your group of students.

NOTE: You're welcome to replace these consequences with ones that might be a better fit for your group of students.

Lead the entire class in the following:

Have students form three teams. If possible, kick off the game with a theme song.

Ladies and gentlemen, you're about to play Face the Consequences. Please take a few moments to select your team's contestant. This person will answer the trivia questions. The catch is that everyone on your team will have to face the consequences if your contestant answers those questions incorrectly. Pause while teams choose contestants. *Will the contestants please come forward? The game is pretty simple. I'll ask the first contestant a question. If the contestant answers*

incorrectly, the team will do the consequence. Then I'll ask the next team the same question.

Play the game until all the questions are asked or everyone faces a consequence.

IN PAIRS
Think of an example from your life of a consequence that you think is fair. Why is it fair? Think of one that, in your opinion, isn't fair. How come?

Let's watch a DVD clip as we think more about why God does some of the things he does.

Show the "Who's a Wimp?" clip on the Grapple DVD.

So there are consequences for our actions when we disobey God. But if God is so powerful, why would he create us with the ability to disobey? Why does God place things in our life that are tempting and/or harmful to us? Let's grapple with that.

GRAPPLE TEAM TIME: 20-25 MINUTES
Break into Grapple Teams. Encourage Grapple Team leaders to check in with kids about their week. Grapple Team leaders will facilitate discussion, using the Grapple Team Guide on pages 83-85. Afterward, students will report what they learned.

GRAPPLE TEAM REPORTS: 10 MINUTES
At the end of Grapple Team Time, match Grapple Teams that chose Option 1 with Grapple Teams that chose Option 2 from page 85. Have teams present their reports.

(If you have an uneven number of teams, simply form one group of three teams for the presentations. If you have only two Grapple Teams, simply do the presentations one team at a time.)

GRAPPLE PRAYER AND CHALLENGE: 5 MINUTES
Read the Grapple Prayer options. Have the class choose one prayer option that everyone will do. Allow students time to pray about what they discovered. Then close in prayer.

Get Ready
For Option 2, distribute copies of maps printed from a mapping website.

Option 1: Still Small Voice
Close your eyes and think about one difficult thing you're currently going through. Ask God to show you where he is in this situation. After a period of reflective silence, ask God what he is trying to say to you through this circumstance. Write down any thoughts or ideas that come to mind.

Option 2: Roadmap of Wisdom
Look at a map, and consider all the different roads and highways and streets feature on that map. Pray for God's guidance, wisdom, and direction in your life, and ask God for strength in following the path and plan he has created for you.

GRAPPLE CHALLENGE

Sometimes when we come into contact with things that harm us, it appears that God is nowhere to be found. We grumble and complain and accuse God of not caring. Occasionally, it looks and feels like God is powerless to stop these things from happening. The truth of the matter is that God desires our hearts. If God didn't give us the freedom to deny him our hearts, then we really couldn't ever truly give him our hearts. God loves us and wants us to love him back.

We messed up the first time and disobeyed God, but God has given us a second chance. The next time you accuse God of not caring for us or not having the power to change our circumstances, I encourage you to stop and thank Jesus for giving you a second chance to give God your whole heart.

WEEKLY GRAPPLE CONNECTION
Grapple Question: Is God a Wimp?
Kids Learn: They Get a Do-Over With Jesus
Dig Into the Bible: Genesis 2:8-17; 3:1-6; Romans 5:18

"Sin and evil are rampant in the world, and I don't see God doing anything about it. In fact, if God is so great, why didn't he just create humans without the capacity to sin?" Teenagers need to know that God loves us and wants us to love him in return. True love requires true freedom to choose. If God controlled our hearts, we could never freely offer them to him. This week, help your kids tackle these questions. Explain to your kids how your desire for their love is similar to God's desire for our love and how that can't be forced or controlled.

- -

GRAPPLE TEAM GUIDE LESSON 8
In your Grapple Team, use this guide to grapple with today's question.

You have just won the lottery. Take a piece of paper and draw or describe your dream home. Where is it? What would the outside/inside look like?

IN PAIRS

Share your picture and describe your dream home. Now imagine coming home to your dream home only to find out that your best friend has played paintball in your house. Now there is bright orange paint in every room. How would you feel? What are the consequences for you and/or your friend?

According to the Bible, God's original intention for humanity was that all of us would live in paradise, a place of peace beyond our wildest imagination.

Read Genesis 2:8-17; 3:1-6

God placed a tree in the garden that was deadly, and God let a crafty serpent live in the garden. Why does God allow bad things into your life?

_____

_____

Why do you think Adam and Eve disobeyed God? How have you noticed the same motivation in your life?

_____

_____

Read Genesis 3:14-19

What were the consequences for the serpent? What's the significance of those consequences?

_____

_____

What were the consequences for the woman? What's the significance of those consequences?

_____

_____

What were the consequences for the man? What's the significance of those consequences?

_____

_____

Read Romans 5:18

In your team, discuss the answers you wrote. Knowing how God set things up (with the tree, the serpent, and the fruit), do you think God was fair or unfair with Adam and Eve? How does God give us a second chance, or a do-over?

GRAPPLE TEAM REPORTS
With your team, choose one of the options below to report what you discovered.

Option 1: New Perspective
Talk about how today's lesson has changed your perspective on sin and its consequences. And then get a new physical perspective: Stand on a table, stand on your head, stretch out on the floor—whatever you want! Hold that position as one member of your team explains how today's lesson has provided a new perspective. Do a "test run" as a team before making your presentation to the other team.

Option 2: Instant Object Lesson
Use whatever you can find around you to create some instant object lessons that explain what you learned today. Get creative!

IS GOD A WIMP?

Ephesians 2:8-9
God saved you by his grace when you believed. And you can't take credit for this; it is a gift from God. Salvation is not a reward for the good things we have done, so none of us can boast about it.

GRAPPLE CHAT
Chat 1: Do we know what kind of fruit Adam and Eve ate in the Garden of Eden?

Chat 2: What is your favorite movie that shows someone getting a second chance?

Chat 3: Find a verse in the Bible that describes God as the God of second chances.

Chat 4: What do you think it would be like to travel to a country in another part of the world? If you've made such a trip, what was it like?

GRAPPLE CHALLENGE
Thank Jesus every day this week for giving you a second chance to give God your whole heart.

NOTES:

_____

_____

_____

_____

_____

_____

_____

_____

_____

WAR AND WELFARE

IS WAR EVER OK?

WAR AND WELFARE

Is War Ever OK?
The Point: I Will Strive for Peace
The Passages: Joshua 8:1-2; Micah 4:1-5; Matthew 5:38-48; 10:34; Romans 12:14-21; Hebrews 10:29-31

GET STARTED
Lesson 9. Is War Ever OK?

GRAPPLE SCHEDULE

5 MINUTES	HANG TIME
10 MINUTES	GRAPPLE CHAT
10-15 MINUTES	GRAPPLE TIME
20-25 MINUTES	TEAM TIME
10 MINUTES	TEAM REPORTS
5 MINUTES	PRAYER & CHALLENGE

SUPPLIES
Bibles, Grapple DVD, DVD player, music CD, CD player, copy of the Grapple Team Guide for each person, paper, pens or pencils

BIBLE BASIS FOR TEACHERS
The Passage: Micah 4:1-5
Micah was a prophet to both Judah and Israel just before Assyria invaded and scattered the tribes throughout the nations. Micah was a contemporary of the prophet Isaiah, although Isaiah prophesied among kings while Micah did not. The people of Israel and Judah during the time of Micah were experiencing a measure of wealth and peace. Accompanying that wealth and peace was an increase in certain social evils. The wealthy were oppressing the poor, worshipping idols, and rejecting God. Because of the people's disobedience, God raised up Assyria to destroy them.

However, Micah also prophesied that God would have mercy on his people and someday raise up a remnant from among them. Historically, this prophecy came true when God raised up a remnant of Israelites after they were defeated by the Assyrians; from the descendents of this remnant, Jesus was born. But there is also a future sense to Micah's prophecy. He is describing a remnant of Christ followers who will "walk in [God's] path" when Christ returns and brings peace to the earth.

How does this relate to the Grapple Question? The issue of war and peace continues to be a hot topic, not only in the culture at-large but also within the

walls of Christianity. There are "peace" churches and there are "justified war" churches. Many teenagers are aware of this tension in their surroundings and in themselves. It's tough to know exactly how we are to approach the issue of war and peace as Christians. This lesson will help kids grapple with this very issue and find some clarity.

How does this connect to Jesus? Jesus said, "God blesses those who work for peace" (Matthew 5:9) and "love your enemies" (Matthew 5:44). Jesus also said, "Don't imagine that I came to bring peace to the earth! I came not to bring peace, but a sword" (Matthew 10:34). There lies much of the confusion. Does Jesus promote peace, or war? This lesson will help teenagers explore the heart of Jesus and, we hope, discover God's will when it comes to this conflict-ridden issue.

GRAPPLE HANG TIME: 5 MINUTES
Play music as kids enjoy snacks and friendship, and then play an opening countdown from the Grapple DVD to wrap up Grapple Hang Time.

GRAPPLE CHAT: 10 MINUTES
Have students form pairs; if you have an uneven number of kids, it's OK to have one trio in the mix. Ask each group to chat about two of the four topics below that relate to today's grapple topic. (Answers in parentheses are samples.)

IN PAIRS
Chat 1: What did David use to kill the giant named Goliath? (A sling and one of five smooth stones from a stream, 1 Samuel 17:50)

Chat 2: Do you have any relative who serves or has served in the armed forces?

Chat 3: What did Samson use to kill 1,000 Philistines? (The jawbone of a donkey, Judges 15:15)

Chat 4: What's your favorite battle movie, and why is it your favorite?

GRAPPLE TIME: 10-15 MINUTES
Get Ready: Cue the Grapple DVD to the "Is War Ever OK?" clip.

Lead the entire class in the following:

Today we're going to play a game called Gorilla, Torch, Poisonous Fruit—which basically is played like Rock, Paper, Scissors. This is how it works: Find a partner and stand back to back. When I count to three (1, 2, 3, jump), turn around and perform one of the three options: Gorilla (pound your chest and roar); Torch (stand straight like a pencil, put your hand on your head, and twiddle your fingers to suggest flames); or Poisonous Fruit (hold your hands in a ball). Gorilla beats Torch by blowing it out. Torch beats Poisonous Fruit by cooking it. Poisonous Fruit beats Gorilla because the gorilla will eat it and die. A tie means you get one more attempt; two ties means you both lose. If you win, find another student who won, and compete against that person. Let's see who will be the last one standing!

IN PAIRS
On a scale of 1 to 10 (1 being quiet pacifist; 10 being violent warrior,) what's your own stance on war and pacifism? Do you believe wars are sometimes necessary and good, or are wars never right? Why?

When students have rated themselves, have them line up to show where they are on the scale.

TELL ALL
What number did you give yourself? What number do you think Christians should be? If God loves peace, why does the Bible have so much killing in it?

Show the "Is War Ever OK?" clip on the Grapple DVD.

There are Christians who believe war is justifiable at times. Other Christians believe violence is wrong under every circumstance. So who is right? And what should we do about it? Is war ever OK? Let's grapple with that!

GRAPPLE TEAM TIME: 20-25 MINUTES
Break into Grapple Teams. Encourage Grapple Team leaders to check in with kids about their week. Grapple Team leaders will facilitate discussion, using the Grapple Team Guide on pages 95-96. Afterward, students will report what they learned.

GRAPPLE TEAM REPORTS: 10 MINUTES
At the end of Grapple Team Time, match Grapple Teams that chose Option 1 with Grapple Teams that chose Option 2 from page 96. Have teams present their reports.

(If you have an uneven number of teams, simply form one group of three teams for the presentations. If you have only two Grapple Teams, simply do the presentations one team at a time.)

GRAPPLE PRAYER AND CHALLENGE: 5 MINUTES
Read the Grapple Prayer options. Have the class choose one prayer option that everyone will do. Allow students time to pray about what they discovered. Then close in prayer.

Get Ready
For Option 1, make sure students have paper and pens or pencils.

Option 1: Prayer Pile
Get in a circle with the rest of your group. Write a prayer to God. Then crumple up the paper with the prayer on it and make a pile of crumpled papers in the middle

of the circle. Choose one crumpled prayer from the pile. Silently pray the words written on the paper, and then ask God to answer the prayer for the person who wrote it.

Option 2: Strong Foundation
Stand up, and close your eyes. While balancing on one foot, silently ask God to help you with a challenging situation you're facing right now. Stay in this position as long as you can—up to two minutes, if possible. Then stand on two feet and ask God to help you be a person who will stand confidently in God's strength.

GRAPPLE CHALLENGE

There are amazing Christians who believe that war is justifiable. There are also amazing Christians who believe that violence of any kind is wrong. And there are amazing Christians who fall somewhere in between. I'm not here to tell you who is right. However, there is common ground for all Christians. Jesus has called us to be peacemakers in the world—to do what we can, when we can, where we can to promote justice and live peaceably with all people. I challenge you to live out Micah 6:8, which tells us to do what is right, to love mercy, and to walk humbly with God.

WEEKLY GRAPPLE CONNECTION
Grapple Question: Is War Ever OK?
Kids Learn: I Will Strive for Peace
Dig Into the Bible: Micah 4:1-5

How does your family feel about war? Ask each family member to give a one-minute response to this question: Is war ever OK? Find out the spectrum of opinions that exist in your family.

The debate about the appropriateness and effectiveness of war will continue. But there is common ground for every Christian: Christ has called us to be peacemakers in the world—to do what we can, when we can, where we can to promote justice and live peaceably with all people. Ask each member of your family to commit to one way of living more peacefully with someone else. Maybe that will mean holding back a retort to a friend or classmate, or making amends with a challenging neighbor, or even—wouldn't this be wonderful—not fighting with a sibling for a week. Even these little efforts can go a long way toward promoting peace in our society.

GRAPPLE TEAM GUIDE LESSON 9

In your Grapple Team, use this guide to grapple with today's question.

Christians believe all kinds of things when it comes to war and resolving conflict. This lesson will not tell you what is right and what is wrong; however, I hope it will clarify for you what you believe, as well as give you some tools to understand those who have differing opinions.

Read Joshua 8:1-2 and Micah 4:1-5

IN PAIRS

What is up with God telling Joshua to kill people? Why would God tell his people to do this? What message about war and peace do you think the passage from Micah is communicating, and why?

Read Matthew 5:38-48

Explain whether or not you think Jesus was for peace or war. If God and Jesus are the same, how can Jesus say this when God told Joshua something so different?

_____

_____

Read Matthew 10:34 and Hebrews 10:29-31

How does the verse from Matthew affect your perception of Jesus? What do you think it means for us that God says, "I will take revenge. I will pay them back"?

_____

_____

Take a minute to write about where you stand on the issue of war and peace.

_____

_____

Read Romans 12:14-21

How does God want us to act toward other people who believe and act differently than we do? What should be our goal? What does it take to put these verses into action in your life?

_____

_____

GRAPPLE TEAM REPORTS

With your team, choose one of the options below to report what you discovered.

Option 1: Project Youth!

With your team, choose your three best ideas about how you could help the youth group learn about today's lesson and put its truths into practice. Be prepared to explain why these truths are important for teenagers to believe and follow.

Option 2: Knowit Poets!

Write a poem or a rap about what you learned today, making every sentence contain the word *war*—or a word that rhymes with it.

IS WAR EVER OK?

Micah 4:4
Everyone will live in peace and prosperity, enjoying their own grapevines and fig trees, for there will be nothing to fear. The Lord of Heaven's Armies has made this promise!

GRAPPLE CHAT
Chat 1: What did David use to kill the giant named Goliath?

Chat 2: Do you have any relative who serves or has served in the armed forces?

Chat 3: What did Samson use to kill 1,000 Philistines?

Chat 4: What's your favorite battle movie, and why is it your favorite?

GRAPPLE CHALLENGE
Be intentional this week to do what is right, to love mercy, and to walk humbly with God.

NOTES:

_____

_____

_____

_____

_____

_____

_____

_____

_____

WAR AND WELFARE

ISN'T IT THEIR FAULT?

WAR AND WELFARE

Isn't It Their Fault?
The Point: I Don't Judge
The Passages: Luke 6:37-42; John 8:1-11; Ephesians 1:4-8; James 4:11-12

GET STARTED
Lesson 10. Isn't It Their Fault?

GRAPPLE SCHEDULE

5 MINUTES	HANG TIME
10 MINUTES	GRAPPLE CHAT
10-15 MINUTES	GRAPPLE TIME
20-25 MINUTES	TEAM TIME
10 MINUTES	TEAM REPORTS
5 MINUTES	PRAYER & CHALLENGE

BIBLE BASIS FOR TEACHERS
The Passage: Luke 6:37-42

Jesus' teaching in this section of the Gospel of Luke is often referred to as the Sermon on the Plain. Like the Sermon on the Mount, Jesus teaches about righteous living, loving one's enemies, and not judging others. In this particular passage, Jesus wants his disciples to understand that true righteousness flows from the heart. Jesus teaches that people with pure hearts, free from hypocrisy, forgive others and guide people toward righteousness. On the other hand, those who are quick to judge and slow to show mercy should spend less time judging and more time examining their own hearts.

How does this relate to the Grapple Question? In a country where teenagers are taught that they have every opportunity to make something of themselves and that people are where they are because they persevered, generosity often falls by the wayside. Sometimes when people encounter someone who is hungry or homeless, their first inclination is to pass judgment rather than show mercy. This lesson will help students grapple with whether or not to show compassion and mercy on people who they think may not deserve it.

How does this connect to Jesus? Jesus consistently reminds us of the rewards of living the way God calls us to live. Jesus also reminds us not to judge others or point a finger at others' shortcomings. Only God knows what motivates people, and ultimately God knows the truth that lies in everyone's heart. Jesus encourages us to give freely, forgive others instead of judging them, and spend some time looking at our own hearts and motivations. When we forgive others, we'll be forgiven, and when we give to others, we will receive even more back (although this shouldn't be our motivation for giving). God does see our

101

sacrifices, and God is pleased when we give of ourselves rather than refusing to be compassionate and merciful because we believe people are where they are because they deserve to be there.

GRAPPLE HANG TIME: 5 MINUTES
Play music as kids enjoy snacks and friendship, and then play an opening countdown from the Grapple DVD to wrap up Grapple Hang Time.

GRAPPLE CHAT: 10 MINUTES
Have students form pairs; if you have an uneven number of kids, it's OK to have one trio in the mix. Ask each group to chat about two of the four topics below that relate to today's grapple topic. (Answers in parentheses are samples.)

IN PAIRS
Chat 1: Find a sin the Bible tells about and the consequence of that sin. (Cain murdered Abel and became a homeless wanderer, Genesis 4.)

Chat 2: Who is the least judgmental person you know? Why is that an accurate description of this person?

Chat 3: Find a person or some people in the Bible who blamed someone else instead of taking the blame themselves. (Potiphar's wife, Genesis 39; the crew on the boat with Jonah, Jonah 1)

Chat 4: What do teenagers most often compare about each other? Would it be grades, cell phones, fashion sense, or something else?

GRAPPLE TIME: 10-15 MINUTES
Get Ready: Cue the Grapple DVD to the "Excuses" clip. Cut five or six pictures out of a teen magazine. The pictures should be of things teenagers would have an opinion about—clothes, cell phones or other technology, celebrities, or sports teams, for example.

Distribute paper and pens. Then lead the entire class in the following:

I'll show you a series of pictures. As I hold up each one, quickly write the first opinion that pops in your head. Don't think about it; just write your first impression or opinion.

Show one picture at a time, allowing about 15 seconds after each one for students to jot down their opinions.

IN PAIRS
Share each of your thoughts with a partner. Note any differences or similarities between what you each wrote.

TELL ALL

What are some things you form quick opinions about? Give an example of a time you kept your opinion to yourself and a time you put your thoughts out there for everyone to hear.

Our brains can form opinions and judgments really quickly. No matter how hard we try to be fair and nonjudgmental, we still have those opinions. Sometimes it's hard to keep them to ourselves. Let's watch a video to see more about this.

Show the "Excuses" clip on the Grapple DVD.

IN PAIRS

How do you feel about helping people when you think they're in a bad situation because of their own choices? Share about a time you felt someone deserved what was happening to him or her.

Isn't it hard to feel sorry for a person who smokes for 50 years and then gets lung cancer? Don't people who gamble all their money away kind of deserve to be poor? When people make poor decisions, shouldn't they have to deal with the consequences? Isn't it their fault that they're in the situation in the first place? Let's grapple with that!

GRAPPLE TEAM TIME: 20-25 MINUTES

Break into Grapple Teams. Encourage Grapple Team leaders to check in with kids about their week. Grapple Team leaders will facilitate discussion, using the Grapple Team Guide on pages 104-106. Afterward, students will report what they learned.

GRAPPLE TEAM REPORTS: 10 MINUTES

At the end of Grapple Team Time, match Grapple Teams that chose Option 1 with Grapple Teams that chose Option 2 from page 106. Have teams present their reports.

(If you have an uneven number of teams, simply form one group of three teams for the presentations. If you have only two Grapple Teams, simply do the presentations one team at a time.)

GRAPPLE PRAYER AND CHALLENGE: 5 MINUTES

Read the Grapple Prayer options. Have the class choose one prayer option that everyone will do. Allow students time to pray about what they discovered. Then close in prayer.

Option 1: Psalms That Pray

Get comfortable, preferably sitting apart from each other. Look through the book of Psalms and find a psalm that connects with a situation you're facing right now. Read the psalm quietly as a prayer to God.

Option 2: Little and Big

Think of "little" sins from this past week that you might have thought were too insignificant to confess. Confess these to God, and ask God to help you change your attitude about all sin—even the "little" sins.

GRAPPLE CHALLENGE

We all make poor decisions—some of us more often than others. Even if we know someone's decision is poor, it's not up to us to pass final judgment on other people's choices. God reserves the right and responsibility to give final judgment on what we do and say. This week, curb your quick judgments of others. When you find yourself feeling judgmental about someone in the coming days, write down your thought and pray about it that night. By holding your tongue, you will be showing grace to those around you.

WEEKLY GRAPPLE CONNECTION
Grapple Question: Isn't It Their Fault?
Kids Learn: I Don't Judge
Dig Into the Bible: Luke 6:37-42

Do you ever find yourself thinking that someone kind of deserves the circumstances they're in? Isn't it hard to feel sorry for a person who smokes for 50 years and then gets lung cancer? Doesn't a person who gambles all his or her money away deserve to be poor? Our brains form opinions and snap judgments very quickly. No matter how hard we try to be fair and nonjudgmental, we still battle those opinions.

We all make poor decisions sometimes—some of us more often than others. But it's not up to us to condemn others for their choices. That's between them and God. Talk to your child about ways to avoid developing judgmental attitudes toward others. Maybe writing down judgmental thoughts—or praying for others, even if they seem to be making poor choices—could help. By holding your tongue, you will be showing grace to those around you.

- -

GRAPPLE TEAM GUIDE LESSON 10

In your Grapple Team, use this guide to grapple with today's question.

Do you ever find yourself thinking that someone kind of deserves to be in a bad situation? For example, let's say your friend asks you for help with his math homework. You assume that he could have done his homework last night but stayed up watching TV instead. It's a little hard to feel sorry for him because it's his own fault that his homework isn't done.

IN PAIRS

When have you felt good about helping someone? How do you usually respond if the person seems to have gotten themselves in a bad situation?

Read John 8:1-11

Write some words that describe Jesus' attitude toward the woman.

_____

_____

IN PAIRS

This woman had clearly sinned, and the crowd thought she deserved a really big punishment. Why did Jesus respond to her the way he did? What can we learn from Jesus about how we should respond to others' sins?

Read Luke 6:37-42

Draw a picture of what this passage means to you.

Based on this passage, what do you think about the question, Isn't it their fault? How does this passage impact the way you would think about someone who is homeless, poor, or in another bad situation?

_____

_____

Read James 4:11-12 and Ephesians 1:4-8

IN PAIRS

Why do we sometimes take over the responsibility of judging people's sins? How does God respond to our sin? Is it ever OK to judge someone else? If so, when? If not, how should we respond instead?

Responding to others' sins without developing a judgmental attitude is more easily said than done. It takes practice to think differently about others. Talk to your Grapple Team about each situation in this chart, and come up with ways you could show grace toward others the way God shows grace to us.

SCENARIO	MY FIRST THOUGHT IS...	A MORE GRACIOUS WAY TO RESPOND IS...
Example: Your friend asks you to show him how to do his math homework.	He probably stayed up all night watching TV and was too lazy to do his homework.	Maybe he had trouble understanding the work. Take some time to explain it to him.
A homeless person on the street asks you for money.		
A classmate is caught stealing a container of milk.		
A family signs up for donated Christmas presents at your church.		

GRAPPLE TEAM REPORTS
With your team, choose one of the options below to report what you discovered.

Option 1: Movie Illustration
Together, think of a scene from a movie that illustrates what you learned today. Be prepared to describe that scene and explain why it illustrates what you've learned.

Option 2: Text It
Write a 140-character text message that you could send to a friend or family member explaining what you learned today.

ISN'T IT THEIR FAULT?

Micah 4:4
Everyone will live in peace and prosperity, enjoying their own grapevines and fig trees, for there will be nothing to fear. The Lord of Heaven's Armies has made this promise!

GRAPPLE CHAT
Chat 1: Find a sin the Bible tells about and the consequence of that sin.

Chat 2: Who is the least judgmental person you know? Why is that an accurate description of this person?

Chat 3: Find a person or some people in the Bible who blamed someone else instead of taking the blame themselves.

Chat 4: What do teenagers most often compare about each other? Would it be grades, cell phones, fashion sense, or something else?

GRAPPLE CHALLENGE
If you find yourself being judgmental this week—stop, write down your thought, and pray about it.

NOTES:

_____

_____

_____

_____

_____

_____

_____

_____

_____

WAR AND WELFARE

SHOULDN'T EVERYONE BE GREEN?

WAR AND WELFARE

Shouldn't Everyone Be Green?
The Point: I Care About My Environment
The Passages: Genesis 1:26-30; Job 37:10-15; Romans 1:20; 8:20-22

GET STARTED
Lesson 11. Shouldn't Everyone Be Green?

GRAPPLE SCHEDULE

5 MINUTES	HANG TIME
10 MINUTES	GRAPPLE CHAT
10-15 MINUTES	GRAPPLE TIME
20-25 MINUTES	TEAM TIME
10 MINUTES	TEAM REPORTS
5 MINUTES	PRAYER & CHALLENGE

SUPPLIES
Bibles, Grapple DVD, DVD player, music CD, CD player, copy of the Grapple Team Guide for each person, paper, pens or pencils, markers, small pieces of masking tape, modeling dough or clay

BIBLE BASIS FOR TEACHERS
The Passage: Genesis 1:26-30
The book of Genesis tells us that God created all that we see in nature and then capped off his wonderful creation by forming Adam and Eve, the first human beings. God gave them (and all the humans who have followed them) a major task: to be stewards of the earth.

This was part of God's perfect plan from the beginning. Notice that after giving Adam and Eve this responsibility, God looked over all he had made, and he saw that it was very good! (Genesis 1:31). And although God gave us the imperative to "reign over" nature, that doesn't mean we are free to destroy and waste the earth's resources. Instead, we are to use them carefully and wisely, for God's purposes.

How does this relate to the Grapple Question? Teenagers already know a lot about environmentalism, but how does that relate to our God-given role as stewards of God's creation? God has entrusted us with the management of this planet, and with God's trust comes a significant responsibility. What does that responsibility look like? In what ways are we called to care for our planet? Students will grapple with questions like these in this lesson.

How does this connect to Jesus? When Adam and Eve sinned they created a rift between us and the environment. God said that because Adam and Eve

disobeyed him "the ground is cursed." God said to Adam, "All your life you will struggle to scratch a living from [the ground]. It will grow thorns and thistles for you" (Genesis 3:17-18). Jesus came to redeem broken relationships—not just between human beings and God, but all broken relationships—including the one between human beings and God's creation. As Christians, we are to follow Jesus by spreading the redemption of all relationships, whether that be relationships with God, other people, ourselves, or God's planet.

GRAPPLE HANG TIME: 5 MINUTES
Play music as kids enjoy snacks and friendship, and then play an opening countdown from the Grapple DVD to wrap up Grapple Hang Time.

GRAPPLE CHAT: 10 MINUTES
Have students form pairs; if you have an uneven number of kids, it's OK to have one trio in the mix. Ask each group to chat about two of the four topics below that relate to today's grapple topic. (Answers in parentheses are samples.)

IN PAIRS
Chat 1: Find two psalms that say that the earth and everything in it belongs to God. (Psalm 24; Psalm 89)

Chat 2: Have you ever gone camping? If so, what was the best part? If not, what would you enjoy most about it?

Chat 3: Discover the names of the four rivers that flowed out of the Garden of Eden. (Pishon, Gihon, Tigris, and Euphrates, Genesis 2)

Chat 4: What items do you and your family recycle most often?

GRAPPLE TIME: 10-15 MINUTES
Get Ready: Cue the Grapple DVD to the "The Ungratefuls" clip.

Read through the activity before your group meets to get a sense of how it would be best to divide your students into rows in your meeting area—for example, something like three rows of five apiece or two rows of four apiece or six rows of four apiece (depending on the size of your group). You'll want students to begin the activity in even rows and columns.

Divide your group into rows. Lead the entire class in the following:

Everybody stand in your assigned rows. I'll read some statements. If a statement is true about you, then follow the instructions, even if it means you have to stand really close to one of your friends! Here we go: Move two spaces to the right if you shower for longer than 15 minutes a day. Move one space to the right if you have picked up a piece of litter and put it in the trash this week. Move two spaces forward if you have ever planted a tree. Move three spaces back if you wear your jeans a couple of times before washing them. Move one space to the left if you recycle regularly. Move one more space to the left if you love hiking. Move one space forward if you know what "leave no trace" means. Move two spaces back if you turn off the lights as you leave a room. Move one space forward if you think God wants us to take care of the environment.

IN PAIRS
Come up with two new things you can easily do to take care of God's creation.

TELL ALL
Being "green" is a popular thing to be right now. But if we were made for heaven, why should we care about what happens here on earth?

Show the "The Ungratefuls" clip on the Grapple DVD.

Is being green a form of "earth worship"? Or is taking care of the earth our God-given responsibility? Does God care either way? Should Christians care? Let's grapple with that!

GRAPPLE TEAM TIME: 20-25 MINUTES
Break into Grapple Teams. Encourage Grapple Team leaders to check in with kids about their week. Grapple Team leaders will facilitate discussion, using the Grapple Team Guide on pages 115-116. Afterward, students will report what they learned.

GRAPPLE TEAM REPORTS: 10 MINUTES
At the end of Grapple Team Time, match Grapple Teams that chose Option 1 with Grapple Teams that chose Option 2 from page 116. Have teams present their reports.

(If you have an uneven number of teams, simply form one group of three teams for the presentations. If you have only two Grapple Teams, simply do the presentations one team at a time.)

GRAPPLE PRAYER AND CHALLENGE: 5 MINUTES
Read the Grapple Prayer options. Have the class choose one prayer option that everyone will do. Allow students time to pray about what they discovered. Then close in prayer.

Get Ready
For Option 2, distribute markers and small pieces of masking tape.

Option 1: Quiet Prayers
Spread out around the room, and get comfortable so you won't be distracted by others. Psalm 143:10 begins with, "Teach me to do your will." Pray that simple phrase over and over, slowly and quietly, and listen for what the Holy Spirit wants to teach you today. Write down any thoughts or ideas that come to mind as you listen.

Option 2: Sticky Situations

Write one of your weaknesses on a small piece of masking tape. Put the tape on your arm, leg, or face. Then pray, asking God to be strong in your weakness. Ask God to speak up for you as your enemy tries to hurt you.

GRAPPLE CHALLENGE

I can think of several reasons for caring about the earth. One reason is that I'm grateful for this masterpiece God made for us. Another reason is that we're made in God's image. God cares for us; we should care for others and for God's creation. But there is a third reason that is just as important. Nature is an awesome way to discover more about God. You want to know if God is powerful? Swim in the ocean, and feel the power of a wave. You want to know if God is big? Climb a mountain; God made that. You want to know if God cares about the details? Look how intricately a flower is put together. Open your eyes next time you are outside and look for evidence of God. You'll discover that God's fingerprints are all around you!

WEEKLY GRAPPLE CONNECTION
Grapple Question: Shouldn't Everyone Be Green?
Kids Learn: I Care About My Environment
Dig Into the Bible: Genesis 1:26-30

People have been focusing a lot lately on how to be "green." What are the best chemical-free detergents to use? How can you cut down on electricity usage? Did you remember to take your reusable bags to the grocery store?

God wants us to take care of the environment because he made it for us to enjoy! God uses nature to show us things about himself. God doesn't want us to worship nature, but by being good stewards of his creation, we can serve and honor God. You want to know if God is powerful? Swim in the ocean and get knocked down by a wave. You want to know if God is big? Climb a mountain. God made that. You want to know if God cares about the details? Look how intricately a flower is put together. Take five minutes out of your day today to look for evidence of God in nature. God's fingerprints are all around you!

GRAPPLE TEAM GUIDE LESSON 11

In your Grapple Team, use this guide to grapple with today's question.

Are you green? Are you anti-green? What does the Bible say about this place where we live? Does it really matter to God?

Read Genesis 1:26-30

IN PAIRS

What, if anything, does being made in the image of God have to do with taking care of the earth? How does the fact that God made us to be fruitful and multiply reflect that we were made in God's image? What responsibilities do you think come with this commission from God?

Read Romans 1:20

Write three ways that nature can teach you about God.

_____

_____

Read Romans 8:20-22
What are some ways the earth has suffered because of humanity's poor choices?

_____

_____

Read Job 37:10-15

IN PAIRS

Why should we or shouldn't we just trust God to take care of things on earth? How do you feel about this statement: "God is ultimately responsible for the good and the bad things that happen to our planet."

God is in control but also gave us responsibility. Where does God's responsibility stop and ours begin?

_____

_____

GRAPPLE TEAM REPORTS

With your team, choose one of the options below to report what you discovered.

Get Ready

For Option 2, distribute modeling dough or clay.

Option 1: Condense It

If you had to summarize today's lesson in only five words, what would they be? As a team, choose the words carefully, and be prepared to explain why you chose them.

Option 2: Sculpt It

Take some modeling dough or clay, and sculpt objects that explain or reveal what you discovered today. Be prepared to interpret your artwork in case you tend to create abstract art!

SHOULDN'T EVERYONE BE GREEN?

Micah 4:4
Everyone will live in peace and prosperity, enjoying their own grapevines and fig trees, for there will be nothing to fear. The Lord of Heaven's Armies has made this promise!

GRAPPLE CHAT
Chat 1: Find two psalms that say that the earth and everything in it belongs to God.

Chat 2: Have you ever gone camping? If so, what was the best part? If not, what would you enjoy most about it?

Chat 3: Discover the names of the four rivers that flowed out of the Garden of Eden.

Chat 4: What items do you and your family recycle most often?

GRAPPLE CHALLENGE
As you walk outside this week, look for evidence of God.

NOTES:

_____

_____

_____

_____

_____

_____

_____

_____

_____

_____

WAR AND WELFARE

ARE WE ALL REALLY THE SAME?

WAR AND WELFARE

Are We All Really the Same?
The Point: I Celebrate Diversity
The Passages: John 4:1-30; Acts 10:1-43; Revelation 7:9-17

GET STARTED
Lesson 12. Are We All Really the Same?

GRAPPLE SCHEDULE

5 MINUTES	HANG TIME
10 MINUTES	GRAPPLE CHAT
10-15 MINUTES	GRAPPLE TIME
20-25 MINUTES	TEAM TIME
10 MINUTES	TEAM REPORTS
5 MINUTES	PRAYER & CHALLENGE

SUPPLIES
Bibles; Grapple DVD; DVD player; music CD; CD player; copy of the Grapple Team Guide for each person; paper; pens or pencils; articles from newspapers, magazines, or websites about people of different races, nationalities, and genders

BIBLE BASIS FOR TEACHERS
The Passage: Revelation 7:9-17
This passage describes a segment of the vision John had on the island of Patmos. In the vision God's saints were standing before the Lamb of God to worship him. Through Jesus Christ—the Lamb of God—God called all people to himself. The vast crowds from every nation, tribe, people, and language described in Revelation 7:9 represent all the families on earth adopted into God's family by Jesus Christ. In eternity, people from every nation, tribe, and language will be in the presence of God to worship him together.

How does this relate to the Grapple Question? In this lesson, students will grapple with the topic of diversity. The Bible teaches that God is impartial when it comes to nationality, gender, cultural background, or skin color. However, many groups often use the Bible to try to excuse their own bigotry and racism. Teenagers at this age are already noticing discrimination occurring between different groups of people. This lesson will help guide students in sorting out these issues and also help them look to Jesus as a model for true acceptance and non-discriminatory love.

How does this connect to Jesus? The Bible says, "God loved the world so much that he gave his one and only son" (John 3:16). And Jesus helped a variety of people. He reached out to the Samaritan woman (see John 4:1-30). He cast out a demon from a girl in the region of Tyre (see Mark 7:24-30). Jesus even healed the son of an "enemy" soldier (see Luke 7:1-10). Jesus reached out to everyone who came to him, and he showed compassion for all people.

GRAPPLE HANG TIME: 5 MINUTES
Play music as kids enjoy snacks and friendship, and then play an opening countdown from the Grapple DVD to wrap up Grapple Hang Time.

GRAPPLE CHAT: 10 MINUTES
Have students form pairs; if you have an uneven number of kids, it's OK to have one trio in the mix. Ask each group to chat about two of the four topics below that relate to today's grapple topic. (Answers in parentheses are samples.)

IN PAIRS
Chat 1: Find at least two different nationalities mentioned in the Bible. (Samaritan, Luke 10; Philistine, 1 Samuel 4)

Chat 2: Do you speak another language besides English? If so, what do you speak? If not, what language would you like to learn, and why?

Chat 3: Find someone in the Bible who was treated differently because of his or her race or nationality. (Samaritan woman, John 4; Canaanite woman, Matthew 15)

Chat 4: If you could live in a different country for three months, which country would you choose, and why?

GRAPPLE TIME: 10-15 MINUTES
Get Ready: Cue the Grapple DVD to the "The Top 5" clip.

Lead the entire class in the following:

Have everyone stand in a circle, facing in.

I've recently decided that I'm going to be in charge of determining what is cool and what is not cool. I see that some of you have long hair [or another characteristic that describes just two or three students, such as color of shirt or style of clothing—don't choose a characteristic such as weight, skin color, intelligence, or anything that could touch too closely to esteem struggles for teenagers]. I know that was cool last week, but I just now decided that having long hair [or other characteristic] aren't going to be cool anymore. So if you have long hair, please step outside the circle. If you are still in the circle, link arms with the person next to you.

I like to think that I'm a pretty fair person, so if you are outside the circle, we'll give you a chance to be part of the group again. Everyone in the circle is going to link arms and try to keep you out, but if you can figure out a way to get in the middle of the circle, then we will accept you again.

Give the students about one minute to try this. If you have time, you can choose a different characteristic and do this again.

TELL ALL
If you were on the outside of the circle, how did it feel to be excluded from the group? If you were part of the circle, how did you feel about keeping someone out?

IN PAIRS
What did you think about excluding people based on their appearance or a specific characteristic? What are some ways you've seen people, races, or nationalities treated differently?

Let's watch a video to see more about this.

Show the "The Top 5" clip on the Grapple DVD.

IN PAIRS
How does God view different cultures? God created so many people with so many differences—does God think that we are equal? Explain. Why do some groups say God chose them to be superior to others?

Regardless of the color of your shirt or your hairstyle today, you are all very much accepted in our group; no one in here is better or worse than the person next to you. People often compare themselves to others based on physical appearance. Sometimes we hear about people who think God chose them or their race as superior to others. What are they basing that on? Does God see different races and cultures differently? Are we really all the same? Let's grapple with that!

GRAPPLE TEAM TIME: 20-25 MINUTES
Break into Grapple Teams. Encourage Grapple Team leaders to check in with kids about their week. Grapple Team leaders will facilitate discussion, using the Grapple Team Guide on pages 125-126. Afterward, students will report what they learned.

GRAPPLE TEAM REPORTS: 10 MINUTES
At the end of Grapple Team Time, match Grapple Teams that chose Option 1 with Grapple Teams that chose Option 2 from page 127. Have teams present their reports.

(If you have an uneven number of teams, simply form one group of three teams for the presentations. If you have only two Grapple Teams, simply do the presentations one team at a time.)

GRAPPLE PRAYER AND CHALLENGE: 5 MINUTES

Read the Grapple Prayer options. Have the class choose one prayer option that everyone will do. Allow students time to pray about what they discovered. Then close in prayer.

Option 1: Prayer Partners

Find a partner to pray with. Talk about troubles you currently face, especially anything connected to today's lesson. Then pray for each other to be able to see your situation from God's perspective.

Option 2: Power Prayers

Clench your fists tight as you imagine using all your power to maintain control over all the different areas of your life. Talk with God, asking for his powerful perspective, and gradually unclench your fists as you give God control. With your hands open and empty, ask God to fill you with his empowering, life-giving Spirit.

GRAPPLE CHALLENGE

Jesus died for every one of us—not just males or females, not just one nationality or another, and not just people with one certain skin color. We are all equal as sinners and in our need of a savior. This week, I encourage you to choose one way to learn about a different culture or nationality, and then think about how you can reach out to individuals from that culture or nationality.

WEEKLY GRAPPLE CONNECTION

Grapple Question: Are We Really All the Same?
Kids Learn: I Celebrate Diversity
Dig Into the Bible: Revelation 7:9-17

People often compare themselves to others based on physical appearance, gender, and age, among other characteristics. The truth is that Jesus died for every one of us—not just males or females, not just one nationality, and not just people with a certain skin color. We're all equal; we're all sinners in need of a savior.

When someone feels afraid of a person who looks different, or feels that his or her culture is superior to another, it's often because that person isn't very well-informed about that other person or culture. With your teenager, brainstorm some ways you can become more educated about other cultures. Think about community events, TV shows or movies, and restaurants that you could explore. Then do one of those ideas this week—and enjoy the fun of expanding your horizons!

GRAPPLE TEAM GUIDE LESSON 12

In your Grapple Team, use this guide to grapple with today's question.

Distribute articles from newspapers, magazines, or websites about people of different races, nationalities, and genders. Have each person in your Grapple Team find an article about a person or group of people different from you in one of those ways.

IN PAIRS

What do you think about the way the writer depicts the people in the article? What are three feelings you have about the person or group, based on what you read?

Read Acts 10:1-43

At the beginning of this passage, Peter and Cornelius both thought there was a difference in how God viewed them. In verse 25, Cornelius started to worship Peter because he thought Peter had a higher status with God. What happened in verses 26-29, and how is that important to you?

_____

_____

IN PAIRS

Read verses 34-35 again. How does God view different cultures and races? What steps do you think God wants all of us to take to relate to different people better? How does God's view of different people affect how you think about people whose appearance, skin color, or culture is different from yours?

Read John 4:1-30

IN PAIRS

Why was the woman surprised that Jesus would talk to her? Why do you think Jesus chose to reach out to her? When the disciples saw Jesus talking to a Samaritan, and when the woman ran back and told people about her interactions with Jesus, how do you think they all responded? How could a similar situation like this occur today? How does hearing this story change the way you think about people who are different from you?

Read Revelation 7:9-17

What do you notice about the people who had gathered in heaven to worship God? How does that affect the way you view different nations and people on earth?

_____

_____

IN PAIRS

Describe a time you've been treated differently because of who you are, whether it was because of your race, gender, nationality, or some other reason. Then describe a time you treated someone else differently because of something that person had no control over.

When people feel afraid of a person of another race or feel that their culture is superior to another culture, it's often because they aren't very well informed about the differences and similarities they have. What are some ways you can become more educated about other cultures? Fill in this chart with ideas:

Events in my community I could attend	
TV shows, movies, books, magazines, or websites I could watch or read	
Foods or restaurants I could try	
People I could talk to	
Other ideas	

GRAPPLE TEAM REPORTS

With your team, choose one of the options below to report what you discovered.

Option 1: Dialogue

Create a scene from your everyday life that includes dialogue involving everyone on your team (or several sample conversations) to demonstrate what you've learned today.

Option 2: Proverb It

Look through the book of Proverbs and find one verse that best connects to what you learned today. If you have enough time, consider finding additional verses.

ARE WE ALL REALLY THE SAME?

Micah 4:4
Everyone will live in peace and prosperity, enjoying their own grapevines and fig trees, for there will be nothing to fear. The Lord of Heaven's Armies has made this promise!

GRAPPLE CHAT
Chat 1: Find at least two different nationalities mentioned in the Bible.

Chat 2: Do you speak another language besides English? If so, what do you speak? If not, what language would you like to learn, and why?

Chat 3: Find someone in the Bible who was treated differently because of his or her race or nationality.

Chat 4: If you could live in a different country for three months, which country would you choose, and why?

GRAPPLE CHALLENGE
This week try to discover one new thing about a different culture or nationality from your own, and then think about how you can reach out to individuals from that culture or nationality.

NOTES:

_____

_____

_____

_____

_____

_____

_____

_____

_____